Ephesians Finding Your Identity in Christ

Bruce BICKEL
&
Stan JANTZ

HARVEST HOUSE™ PUBLISHERS

EUGENE, OREGON

Cover by Left Coast Design, Portland, Oregon

Cover photo by Londie G. Padelsky, Mammoth Lakes, California

CHRISTIANITY 101 is a registered trademark of Bruce Bickel and Stan Jantz. Harvest House Publishers, Inc., is the exclusive licensee of the federally registered trademark CHRISTIANITY 101.

EPHESIANS: FINDING YOUR IDENTITY IN CHRIST
Copyright © 2003 by Bruce Bickel and Stan Jantz
Published by Harvest House Publishers
Eugene, Oregon 97402
www.harvesthousepublishers.com

Library of Congress Cataloging-in-Publication Data

Bickel, Bruce, 1952–
    Ephesians: finding your identity in Christ / Bruce Bickel and Stan Jantz.
        p. cm. — (Christianity 101®)
    ISBN-13: 978-0-7369-0792-7
    ISBN-10: 0-7369-0792-0 (pbk.)
    Product # 6907920
    1. Bible. N.T. Ephesians—Commentaries. 2. Bible. N.T. Ephesians—Study and teaching. I. Jantz, Stan, 1952– II. Title. III. Series.
    BS2695.53 .B53 2003
    227'.507—dc21

                                                        2002010616

Printed in the United States of America

07 08 09 10 11 / DP-KB / 10 9 8 7 6 5

Contents

A Note from the Authors

*D*on't you wish sometimes that everything you needed to know about living the Christian life was contained in a concise, simple book? And don't you wish that after you read that book, everything about your relationship to God would fall into place without any trouble or struggle?

Unfortunately, you're never going to find such a book, so you may as well stop looking. And you're never going to get around the fact that living your life with God will always have its share of complications and challenges. That's not to say that there aren't a whole bunch of great books out there that will help you live the Christian life, struggles and all. Obviously, the Bible—God's personal message of love to you—has to be on the top of your list. Reading God's Word every day needs to be a priority.

But if you were trying to find a relatively short book that you could read again and again and get something fresh out of every time, then you couldn't do much better than the book of Ephesians. We won't tell you that Ephesians is a simple book. It deals with some very *basic* things you need to know to grow as a Christian, but it is pretty lofty (William Barclay said that Ephesians contained the highest level of New Testament thought). Get ready to stretch your spiritual muscles.

Just a Little Help

The last thing the world needs is another commentary on Ephesians. That's why we've taken a different approach in this guide to Ephesians. Let's face it. There are lots of scholarly books that will give you the technical theological concepts behind the book of Ephesians. If you want to dig into the original language of Paul's letter, you can find a commentary that will bring out the meanings of the Greek words. But if you simply want a book to help you understand Ephesians and what it means to you personally, then this is the book you need to read.

Our approach to Bible study is very simple. We won't get in the way of your own personal study, but we will guide and encourage you along the way. In the first two chapters, you will learn the historical, cultural, and theological settings for Ephesians. Here we'll give you the central focus and the major themes of the book. In the other 11 chapters, we will walk through Ephesians with you, helping you to understand what it means—and what it means to you. We are confident that the book of Ephesians will change the way you live as you discover the wonderful things God has done to help you live the Christian life.

Christianity 101 Bible Studies

This Bible study on Ephesians is part of a series called Christianity 101 Bible Studies. We've designed this series to combine the biblical content of a commentary with the life applications of a Bible study. By reading this book and answering the questions, you will learn the basics of what you need to know so you will get more meaning from the Bible. Not only that, but you will be able to apply what the Bible says to your everyday Christian life.

And just in case you want even more help in your study of God's Word, we have listed some books that were helpful to us in our study of Ephesians. You'll find these at the end of the book in a section called "Dig Deeper." In addition, we have put together an on-line resource exclusively for users of the Christianity 101 Bible Studies series. All you have to do is click on www.christianity101online.com (see page 165 for details).

This Book Is for You

Maybe this is your first time using a resource for studying the Bible, or maybe you are an experienced Bible student. Either way, we think this book is for you if...

- Reading the Bible is sometimes a little confusing for you. You get the overall picture, but you want additional information and insights to help you better understand how the Bible fits into your life and the world around you.

- You enjoy reading the Bible, but you don't think you're getting enough out of it. Sometimes it seems like the Bible isn't much more than a history book or a collection of wise sayings. You want the Bible to come alive and change the way you live.

- You and a few friends want to study a book of the Bible together, and you figure Ephesians is a good place to start. You don't want a Bible study that will force you all to come to the same conclusions. You want a book that will give everyone room to think for themselves.

A Few Suggestions Before You Begin

We're ready to give you a little help, but we want to stay in the background. Remember, we aren't your teachers. We are more like trail guides explaining a few things and showing you some points of interest along the way. The Holy Spirit is your teacher, and He's the best there is. He will show you everything you need to know about Ephesians and how it applies to your Christian life.

> *But we know these things because God has revealed them to us by his Spirit, and his Spirit searches out everything and shows us even God's deep secrets* (1 Corinthians 2:10).

We are convinced that as you study the book of Ephesians, God will speak directly to you through His Word and through the inner voice of the Holy Spirit. Our prayer is that your study of Ephesians will change your life as you understand who you are in Jesus.

If You Are Studying Ephesians on Your Own

- Have your Bible open to Ephesians.

- Pray and ask God to help you understand His Word.

- Before you begin, read Ephesians all the way through to get an overview. Don't worry about getting all the meaning and application.

- As you work through each chapter in this guide, try to understand the themes of Ephesians as well as the context in the larger scope of the Bible.

- Write out your answers to the questions and exercises at the end of each chapter. Writing your thoughts down will reinforce what you are learning.

- Thank God for the wonderful riches of His Word and His provisions for your life.

If You Are Studying Ephesians in a Group

- Come prepared by doing everything suggested for individual study.

- Be a willing participant in the discussions, but don't dominate the conversation.

- Encourage and affirm the other people in your group as they talk. Sometimes the best way to do this is to make eye contact and nod your head in an approving manner.

- Be open and honest in your answers. If you don't understand something, admit it! Someone else may have the answer you're looking for.

- Sharing what a particular passage means to you is okay, but first you should try to discover what it means to everyone. Remember, biblical truths aren't different for different people.

- If someone shares something confidential, keep it in the group. At the same time, avoid turning your group Bible study into a gossip session.

- Pray for the other members of your group on a regular basis. Here's how Paul prayed for a group of Christians in his day:

So we have continued praying for you ever since we first heard about you. We ask God to give you a complete understanding of what he wants to do in your lives, and we ask him to make you wise with spiritual wisdom. Then the way you live will always honor and please the Lord, and you will continually do good, kind things for others. All the while, you will learn to know God better and better (Colossians 1:9-10).

That's our prayer for you as well, so let's get started.

Chapter 1

The letter to the Ephesians is a marvelously concise, yet comprehensive, summary of the Christian good news and its implications. Nobody can read it without being moved to wonder and worship, and challenged to consistency of life.

—*John R.W. Stott*

Your True Identity

Everybody is concerned about identity these days. People want to know who you are, especially if you want to do something important like drive a car, cash a check, or board a plane. Without some kind of document that identifies you with a picture and a description of your physical features, you are limited in what you can do.

You have another kind of identity that is much different than a little laminated card you carry in your wallet. This kind of ID has nothing to do with who you are on the *outside* and everything to do with who you are on the *inside*. This true identity is all about your essential self and those characteristics that make you uniquely you. The book of Ephesians will help you discover your true identity.

A Lofty Letter for Committed Christians

*A*ll of us know who we are on the outside, but most of us wonder from time to time who we are on the inside. That's natural. It's part of being human. But where do you go to find out? Do you watch *Oprah* a lot, hoping one of those special guest psychologists will give you a clue? Do you take an instant personality profile test that tells you who you are after you've answered a series of questions? Or do you spend years in therapy talking to someone who may be just as confused as you are?

You can try these things, but we have a much better idea: Study the book of Ephesians. In this short New Testament book, you will find everything you need to know about your true identity. Don't get us wrong. You will not discover if you are a dominant personality or the life of the party. You're not going to uncover repressed memories from your childhood. No, you are going to learn something much more important. You are going to find out who you are in Jesus Christ.

If you are a Christian, you automatically have a new identity. The Bible puts it this way:

> *What this means is that those who become Christians become new persons. They are not the same anymore, for the old life is gone. A new life has begun!* (2 Corinthians 5:17).

That's the good news. The bad news is that if you don't know what your identity in Jesus is all about, you're not going to experience all of the benefits and blessings your new life has to offer. That's why studying the book of Ephesians may just be the best decision you've made in quite some time.

A Recipe for the Christian Life

Pound for pound, verse for verse, the book of Ephesians is one of the most profound, powerful, and practical books in the entire Bible. It's written to "faithful followers of Christ Jesus" (1:1) who want to know what this thing called the Christian life is all about. As a Christ follower (that's another way to say *Christian*), you have an identity that is so amazing and so glorious, you will hardly believe it. Your identity started in eternity past, and it will continue into eternity future. And right now it defines who you are. The more you read Ephesians and the better you understand your identity in Christ, the better you will know the real you.

You want identity? You've come to the right place. You want to know how to live the Christian life? You've found the recipe.

*E*phesians at a *G*lance

Author:	Paul the Apostle
Date written:	A.D. 60 or 61
Written to:	The church at Ephesus and all believers everywhere
Type of book:	An epistle, or letter
Setting:	Paul lived in Ephesus for three years, but he wrote this letter while in prison in Rome.
Purpose:	Paul teaches believers their true identity in Christ and reveals the mystery of the body of Christ, also known as the church, in which we are all one.
Major themes:	We belong to Christ (1:3), the Holy Spirit is our guarantee (1:14), and we can share in God's power (1:19).

Dr. R.C. Sproul calls Ephesians "a recipe for godly living." Every recipe includes *ingredients* and *instructions,* and that's exactly what Ephesians has. The first part of the book gives us the *ingredients of belief.* This involves knowing God and what He has done for us in Christ. The second part of the book gives us the *instructions for behavior.* This involves doing what God wants us to do.

Before we dig into this amazing book, we need to know a little about the person who wrote it. You will better understand Ephesians if you first know what's going on behind the scenes.

All About Paul

Next to Jesus, there is no one more important to Christianity than the apostle Paul. He was the greatest missionary the world has ever seen. Paul not only carried the Gospel—or *Good News*—of Jesus Christ to the far reaches of the Roman Empire in the first century but also established the foundation of the Christian belief system through his letters to churches and individuals. Ephesians is one of nine letters Paul wrote to the young churches in Asia Minor (present-day Turkey), Greece, and Italy. Paul also wrote four letters to individuals. Nearly 2000 years after he wrote his letters, churches and individuals around the world still read and study them in great detail.

How did it happen that one man has had such a profound influence on the Christian faith? The answer will surprise you.

A Roman Tent Maker

Paul (his Roman name) was born Saul (his Jewish name) in Tarsus, an important commercial city with two distinctions that were to play a major role throughout Paul's life:

- Tarsus was the capital of a Roman province, and Paul was a Roman citizen by birth. On more than one occasion when he was preaching the Gospel, Paul relied on his citizenship to prevent a severe beating at the hands of Roman officials (Acts 22:25-29). In addition, Paul's Roman citizenship acted like a universal passport, allowing him to travel freely throughout the Empire.

The Letters of Paul

To Churches	Location	Present Day	Date
Romans	Rome	Italy	A.D. 57
1 and 2 Corinthians	Corinth	Greece	55-57
Galatians	Galatia	Turkey	49
Ephesians	Ephesus/ Asia Minor	Turkey	60 or 61
Philippians	Philippi	Greece	61
Colossians	Colossae	Turkey	60
1 and 2 Thessalonians	Thessalonica	Greece	51-52

To Individuals	Relationship to Paul	Date
1 and 2 Timothy	Disciple and close friend	64-67
Titus	Paul's representative to Crete	64
Philemon	Member of the church at Colossae	60

- Tarsus was known for the production of *cilicium,* a cloth made of goat's hair that was commonly used to make sails, awnings, and tents. Paul learned the trade of tent making and used it to support himself when he became a missionary.

A Complete Jew

Sometime between the ages of 13 and 20, Paul moved to Jerusalem, where he began training to be a rabbi under master teacher Gamaliel. Gamaliel's grandfather had founded the Pharisaic school, whose teachings influence Judaism to this day. "At his feet," Paul once said to a crowd of Jews, "I learned to follow our Jewish laws and customs very carefully. I became very zealous to honor God in everything I did, just as all of you are today" (Acts 22:3). Paul was the complete Jew.

Saul the Persecutor

Saul the zealot became Saul the persecutor:

> *And I persecuted the followers of the Way [Christians], hounding some to death, binding and delivering both men and women to prison* (Acts 22:4).

The most famous example of Saul's involvement in the persecution and killing of Christians occurred when Stephen, one of the leaders of the early church, became the church's first martyr. A *martyr* is someone who is put to death for professing their faith. *Martyr* comes from the Greek word for *witness*. According to The Voice of the Martyrs, an estimated 165,000 people were martyred in various parts of the world in the year 2000.

Saul stood by as Stephen was stoned to death (Acts 8:1). Following Stephen's martyrdom, Saul became the church's greatest enemy. He was a man possessed, "uttering threats with every breath." He was determined to "destroy the Lord's followers" (Acts 9:1). Then something happened that dramatically changed Saul and the church forever.

From Saul to Paul

Leave it to Jesus to choose the least-likely candidate to carry out His message. Acts 9 tells the dramatic story of Saul's conversion from chief persecutor of the church to

its main missionary. It happened in a flash (literally) on
the road to Damascus, where Saul was going to arrest
more Christians. Saul was knocked to the ground by a
"brilliant light from heaven," and a voice called out:
"Saul! Saul! Why are you persecuting me?"

When Saul asked who it was, Jesus replied, "I am Jesus,
the one you are persecuting" (Acts 9:5). From that point
forward Saul was spiritually transformed, and he became
the Lord's "chosen instrument" to take the Good News
of Jesus "to the Gentiles and to kings, as well as to the
people of Israel" (Acts 9:15). His conversion sent shock-
waves throughout the church. Many refused to believe
that God could use such a horrible enemy of Christianity.

When the Lord Calls Your Name Twice

Throughout the history of the Bible, God called upon a few
people—usually the most unlikely people—to do a great work
for Him, and when He did, God often spoke their name twice:

Names	Reference	What God Asked Them to Do
"Abraham! Abraham!"	Genesis 22:11	Sacrifice his son, Isaac
"Moses! Moses!"	Exodus 3:4	Lead God's people out of Egypt
"Samuel! Samuel!"	1 Samuel 3:4	Become the first prophet of Israel
"Saul! Saul!"	Acts 9:4	Become a great missionary

The lesson here is that if you ever hear God call your name
twice, be prepared to do something great for Him. If it's just your
parents or your spouse calling your name out twice, be prepared to take out the garbage.

This should be a lesson to all of us. How many times have you written somebody off because you thought they were too horrible or too evil to ever change? Doing this with famous people (especially terrorists) is easy, but what about some of the people you know personally? Have you given up spiritually on a neighbor, a friend, or someone you know casually because you think they have turned their back on God? Have you stopped praying for someone (or maybe you never prayed in the first place) because you think they are beyond being saved?

Who do we think we are? Who are we to judge whether God can save and use someone or not? If God didn't give up on Saul, the church's greatest enemy, He won't give up on anybody—and neither should we. Jesus said:

> But I say, love your enemies! Pray for those who persecute you! In that way, you will be acting as true children of your Father in heaven (Matthew 5:44-45).

The Believers Scatter

Just before Jesus left the earth and ascended into heaven, He gave this command:

> But when the Holy Spirit has come upon you, you will receive power and will tell people about me everywhere—in Jerusalem, throughout Judea, in Samaria, and to the ends of the earth (Acts 1:8).

Seven weeks later the Holy Spirit came upon the believers on the day of Pentecost (Acts 2:1), and they started witnessing to people in Jerusalem. Led by the powerful preaching of the apostle Peter, the church grew quickly. However, for the most part, the believers remained in and around Jerusalem. Only after Stephen's death and the intense persecution that followed were the believers forced into Judea and Samaria (Acts 8:1).

We may not always understand God's ways, and when we do, we usually figure them out after the fact. The growth of the early church is a good example. Jesus told the believers to go to the ends of the earth, but they were playing it safe in Jerusalem. Then the persecution began, and God used it to push His children out of their comfort zone just like a mother eagle forces her babies to jump out of the nest and fly.

Paul the Missionary

As we look back on these events in the early church, we can see why God chose to convert Paul at this particular time. God needed someone to take the Good News of Jesus Christ to the ends of the earth. And that meant He needed someone to go out from the Jewish-centered church of Jerusalem to help pioneer the Gentile church of the Roman world, including Ephesus. Because of his Roman citizenship, Paul was the perfect choice. Here's what Paul wrote:

> *For I am, by God's grace, a special messenger from Christ Jesus to you Gentiles. I bring you the Good News* (Romans 15:15-16).

In the span of about 30 years, Paul took four missionary journeys and carried the Good News throughout the Roman world, establishing churches and encouraging believers. One of his favorite places was Ephesus, a world-class city that became one of the most influential Christian centers in the world.

■ ■ ■

Study the Word

1. Read 2 Corinthians 5:17. In what way do Christians become "new persons"? What happens to the "old life"?

   If you are a Christian, describe what happened when your new life began.

2. Why might knowing who you are in Christ be a pre-requisite for doing what He wants you to do?

3. What is a "tent-making" ministry? What advantages might it offer to ministry and missions?

4. How might Paul's extensive knowledge of Jewish laws and customs have helped him in his Christian life? What could you do to learn more about the culture that gave birth to Christianity?

5. Paul's life is a classic illustration of how God can dramatically turn a life around. Give an example of someone you know whose life as a Christian is completely different from his or her life before Christ. Feel free to use your own life as an example.

6. Describe a time when God used negative circumstances to push you out of your comfort zone. What
   was the long-term effect on your spiritual life?

7. Read Romans 8:28. How does this verse apply to
   Paul's life? How does it apply to yours?

Chapter 2

I think the gospel was more effective in this area than in any place at any time in the history of the world. I believe the Ephesian church was the highest church spiritually.

—J. Vernon McGee

A Spiritual Heritage

Did you know that your city has a spiritual heritage? How do you think all of those churches and ministries got there? They didn't just spring up on their own. They were founded by people with a heart for God and a passion to take the Good News of Jesus Christ to the corner of the world where you live.

The city of Ephesus could be a model for your city. Though it was an ancient city, it shared many similarities with our modern times. It had all the characteristics of a city filled with darkness and sin, and yet the light of Christ was unmistakable, thanks to the Ephesian church and the persistent ministry of Paul.

To help you better understand how the truths of Ephesians apply to your life, you need to take a look at the spiritual history of Ephesus. That's what we're going to do in this chapter.

An Ancient City for Modern Times

*T*he city of Ephesus was one of the most important and impressive cities in the entire Roman Empire. Located on the western coast of Asia Minor, Ephesus was a great cultural and religious center. Millions of people lived in Asia Minor, and Ephesus was the largest city, with as many as 250,000 residents. In fact, Ephesus was second in importance only to Rome in the entire Empire. It was so popular and inviting that the Roman emperors used to vacation there.

Ephesus and the Temple of Artemis

If Rome was the New York City of its day, then Ephesus was Las Vegas. That might be stretching it a bit, but Ephesus was a big tourist center, mainly because of its great Temple of Artemis, the Greek goddess of fertility (the counterpart to Diana in the Roman pantheon of gods). The people of Ephesus were crazy about Artemis, so they constructed a temple with 127 majestic columns that was four times larger than the Greek Parthenon in Athens. The Temple of Artemis was one of the Seven Wonders of the Ancient World.

Tourists and pilgrims alike flocked to Ephesus to take in the culture and see the temple. There was a big souvenir business in Ephesus, and the most popular items were replicas of the Temple of Artemis and shrines to the goddess herself made out of silver. In fact, the economy of Ephesus was largely driven by the tourist trade and especially by the sale of these temple souvenirs.

As the church in Ephesus grew and people believed in Jesus rather than Artemis, sales for the silver souvenirs began to shrink. The leader of the silversmiths in Ephesus was a man named Demetrius, who blamed Paul for the significant loss of business. At a meeting of the Ephesus Chamber of Commerce, Demetrius said, "As you have seen and heard, this man Paul has persuaded many people that handmade gods aren't gods at all. And this is happening not only here in Ephesus but throughout the entire province" (Acts 19:26). A riot broke out, all because those pesky Christians persuaded the Ephesians to follow the one true God rather than their fake silver gods.

When you think about it, our culture today isn't all that different from ancient Ephesus. We may not have a temple to the goddess of fertility, but we do have temples and shrines where we give our money and allegiance, only we call them stadiums, theaters, casinos, malls, and office buildings. People have forsaken the one true God in order to pay tribute to the gods who live in these structures: money, success, sports, prestige, power, celebrity—the list goes on. We may not give these things names like Artemis or Diana, but we worship them just the same. Only God can turn people from these idols, and the way He does it is through the witness and knowledge and love of people just like you.

Paul Visits Ephesus

For years, Paul had wanted to go to Ephesus. He knew that it would be a strategic place to establish a church that would in turn reach out into the other cities of Asia Minor. Paul wasn't able to travel to Ephesus until the end of his second missionary journey (around A.D. 52), and he only stayed long enough to debate with the Jews in the synagogue (Acts 18:19-20). Only after his third missionary journey did Paul return to Ephesus, and this time he stayed for a while—three years, to be exact. This was the longest time Paul ever spent in one city. He knew that Ephesus and the believers there would play a key role in the advancement of the Gospel.

The Church at Ephesus

Paul was a tiger. He loved a rousing debate. He was passionate about his faith in Jesus Christ. The same qualities that propelled Paul to success as a Jewish zealot and persecutor of Christians—his keen mind and his obstinate personality—were now being channeled into his desire to tell the world about Jesus. Thomas Cahill writes in *Desire of the Everlasting Hills:*

The combination of intellectual and emotional relentlessness that constituted Paul's personality made this unlikely man the perfect vehicle for this moment in the development of the Jesus Movement.

$\mathcal{P}$aul and $\mathcal{A}$pollos

From the time Paul visited Ephesus at the end of his second missionary journey to his return at the beginning of his third journey, something interesting happened. An eloquent and gifted public speaker by the name of Apollos had arrived in Ephesus. Eager to share what he knew about the Scriptures, Apollos wowed the crowds with his stirring speeches. There was only one problem. His knowledge was incomplete. His preaching was based on the Old Testament and John the Baptist.

The leaders of the church had to take Apollos aside and explain that he needed more training, especially in the knowledge about Jesus Christ. Contrast this with Paul, who made sure his knowledge about the Scriptures and Jesus was thorough. After his conversion, Paul took 14 years to prepare for his service as a missionary of the Good News of Christ. By the time he arrived in Ephesus, he was ready to accurately explain the Word of God.

The first place Paul headed upon his arrival in Ephesus in A.D. 53 was the synagogue, where he "preached boldly" for three months (Acts 19:8). After encountering some opposition, Paul and his fellow believers left the synagogue and set up shop at the lecture hall of Tyrannus, a public place where people came to study and debate. Paul spoke here for two years for up to five hours a day. As Paul preached daily, he reached two kinds of people:

- *unbelievers* who did not know the truth about Jesus and the Resurrection

- *believers* who wanted to learn more about their faith from a master Bible teacher

J. Vernon McGee writes: "The people of Ephesus heard more Bible teaching from Paul than did any other people, which is the reason he could write to them the deep truths contained in this epistle."

From Ephesus to Prison

The three years Paul spent in Ephesus were among the most productive of his missionary career. He saw the believers grow in number and in spiritual maturity. Paul must have been very pleased, but he had to move on. Paul departed for Corinth in Greece, where he spent the winter of A.D. 55–56 and wrote his letter to the Romans. From Corinth, Paul headed for Jerusalem, where he was greeted with fierce opposition. The Jewish leaders there considered Paul to be a traitor and an enemy. They convinced the people that he was against their religious system and the Temple.

Sure enough, things in Jerusalem got out of control, a mob formed, and Paul was about to be killed when the Roman army stepped in. The commander and his regiment took Paul away for his own safety. Paul remained in protective custody for a total of four years. For the first two years, Paul was in the custody of two Roman governors, Felix and his successor, Festus. Paul finally used the privilege of his Roman citizenship and asked for a hearing before Caesar. Festus had to honor his request, so Paul was transferred to Rome, where he was imprisoned for another two years waiting for his appearance before Emperor Nero.

$\mathscr{P}$aul and $\mathscr{P}$rison

Paul knew what it was like to be beaten, whipped, and stoned to within an inch of his life, all because he preached the Good News of Jesus (2 Corinthians 11:16-33). Paul was in prison so many times he lost count. Sometimes it was overnight, and sometimes it was as long as two years. Paul wrote his letter to the Ephesians while he was imprisoned in Rome. In fact, he wrote four letters from his Roman prison: Philippians, Ephesians, Colossians, and Philemon (that's why they're called the Prison Epistles).

God was gracious to Paul during these years. Even though he was in chains and guarded by soldiers, he was confined to a "house" where he could receive visitors and write his letters. Still, this wasn't the Roman Holiday Inn. It was a prison. The place was probably dark and damp, and the food wasn't exactly gourmet. Worse, Paul's future was uncertain. But Paul knew why he was there:

> And I want you to know, dear brothers and sisters, that everything that has happened to me here has helped to spread the Good News. For everyone here, including all the soldiers in the palace guard, knows that I am in chains because of Christ. And because of my imprisonment, many of the Christians here have gained confidence and become more bold in telling others about Christ (Philippians 1:12-14).

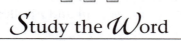

$\mathcal{S}$tudy the $\mathcal{W}$ord

1. To the best of your knowledge, give a summary of the spiritual history of your city. If you need more information, where could you get it?

2. Give an example of a shrine or an idol in your city that is contrary to the person of Christ and the truths of Scripture. What message do Christians have for those who worship that idol or frequent that shrine? How might that message be most effectively communicated?

   What shrines or idols in our own lives take our attention away from Jesus? How can we maintain purity and a clear focus on Him?

3. Read Galatians 1:15–2:1 and Acts 18:24-28. Compare the study methods of Paul and Apollos.

Read 2 Timothy 2:15. Which man—Paul or Apollos—better exemplified this advice? Why?

Now, think about your own knowledge of "the word of truth." How prepared are you to correctly explain the Scriptures to believers? To skeptics? List three things you can begin doing that will help you "be a good worker, one who does not need to be ashamed."

4. What dangers confront a church where the truth of the Bible is not taught in a systematic way?

5. Read Matthew 22:37. Compare and contrast loving God and knowing God.

Read Romans 12:1-2. How do worshiping God and knowing God affect each other?

6. Is knowing the national and local laws and ordinances regarding the free expression of worship and your belief in God and the Bible important? Why or why not? Should you obey those laws if they prevent you from witnessing or worshiping in the public square? Why or why not?

7. Read 2 Corinthians 11:16-33. Why do you think Paul
    decided to "boast" in this way? Was he frustrated,
    proud, or simply trying to make a point? If he was
    trying to make a point, what was it?

Chapter 3

So then, in this world without Christ, there is nothing but disunity. That disunity is not God's purpose, but it can become a unity only when all things are united in Christ.

—*William Barclay*

The Church Is You

Ah, the church. It's supposed to be the body of Christ, but sometimes it seems more like a rerun of *Family Feud*. Why does this marvelous spiritual organization, established by God Himself to function as an extension of Jesus Christ on earth, have so many problems?

The quick answer is *people*. A church is a "body of believers," and there has yet to be a perfect believer. But God hasn't given up on the church. Far from it. God has made perfectly clear in His Word—especially in the book of Ephesians—that He has chosen the church to bring His peace, hope, and love to a hurting world.

Never forget that the church isn't a building. The church is *you*. That's what we're going to discover in this chapter as we dig into Ephesians.

A Letter for All Who Follow Christ

Ephesians 1:1-2

*L*et's set the scene for how and why Ephesians was written. Picture Paul in prison, thinking about his fellow believers in Ephesus. He decides to write them a letter. He hasn't been with them for a few years, but the memory of their spiritual growth is fresh. Paul hasn't heard about any problems or controversies. The church is functioning well. So what does Paul tell them?

In a word, Paul tells the Ephesians what their new identity in Christ really means. He tells them about the church—not only their local body of believers but also the church universal, the body of Christ. John Stott calls Ephesians "the gospel of the church." In just six chapters, Ephesians reveals God's eternal "secret plan" to create the

church, a new "society" of believers, through and in
Christ.

- In the first three chapters of Ephesians, Paul writes
  about the heavenly calling of the church. These
  chapters are *doctrinal* in nature.

- In the second three chapters of Ephesians, Paul
  writes about the earthly conduct of the church.
  These chapters are *practical* in nature.

The Unity of the Church in Christ

God's purpose has always been to establish the church
in order to bring all things together in Christ. The unity
of the church stands in stark contrast to the disunity of the
world. William Barclay points out several tensions and
conflicts we see all around us every day:

- nation wars against nation

- man is divided from man

- Jews and Gentiles don't get along

- ideas conflict with other ideas

There's no way to get away from this disunity. You
couldn't isolate yourself if you tried, and even if you
could succeed in getting away from all the conflict in the
world, you would discover the war going on in your own
nature between your desire to do good and your desire
for no good (see Romans 7:15-25, where Paul describes
this war).

And then there are conflicts on a cosmic scale:
between the powers of good and evil, between God and

Satan, and between God and man. The only way a world in conflict can be brought together is through Jesus Christ. And the way Jesus brings people together in Him is through the church. That's the central message of Ephesians.

The Major Themes of Ephesians

You're going to see three themes running through the book of Ephesians, each one related to the central message of the unity of the church in Christ:

1. We belong to Christ (1:3).

2. The Holy Spirit is our guarantee (1:14).

3. We can share in God's power (1:19).

How wonderful that nearly 2000 years later, we have the opportunity to read this lofty letter Paul wrote to the believers in Ephesus and the entire region of Asia Minor. He had taught these growing Christians in person for three years, building them up in their faith. He had dished out spiritual meat, and they were hungry for more. He knew they were ready to receive the deep truths about God.

And so we have a book that contains some of the most profound truths in the entire Bible. In this one letter are insights into the very mind of God, revelations of a "secret plan" that stretches from eternity past into eternity future. The church at Ephesus was ready to hear about the church universal, the body of Christ. With some serious study and the help of the Holy Spirit, they were able to understand what Paul was writing about.

The same goes for you. Are you ready to receive the deep truths of God? Are you anxious to move from the baby stage of your Christian life, where milk is about all you can handle, to the adult stage, where you are ready for something substantial to chew on? Then you're ready for Ephesians.

You see, the secrets in Ephesians aren't just *for* you; they are *about* you as well. They are about the things God has done for you in Christ, and they are about the things God wants you to do once you learn the secrets. It's as if God is cupping His hand around your ear and whispering, "I've got some important things to tell you that are going to change your life."

God Is Speaking to You

Every time you read the Bible, God is speaking personally to you. Never forget that the Bible is much more than a collection of ancient books and letters. It is God's personal message to you, telling you how much He loves you and wants a relationship with you forever.

A Letter for All Who Follow Christ (1:1-2)

We've been saying all along that Ephesians is a lofty letter. In keeping with the high purpose of his letter, Paul gets right to the point. He identifies himself as one who has been "chosen by God to be an apostle of Christ Jesus." Paul knew what it was like to be chosen by God. He wasn't seeking God on that road to Damascus. Paul was intent on destroying Christians. God clearly chose Paul when He blinded him with the light of Jesus.

From: Paul the Apostle

In the New Testament, an apostle was one who saw Jesus after His Resurrection and received a special commission from Him. Because Paul had a personal encounter with Jesus, he could call himself an apostle. Consequently, his words carry apostolic weight and authority.

To: God's Holy People

Paul addressed his letter to "God's holy people in Ephesus." The words "in Ephesus" do not appear in some early manuscripts. It's likely that the letter was written to Gentiles throughout Asia Minor. Paul didn't personalize the letter at all, which seems odd considering his close relationship with the believers at Ephesus (remember, he stayed in the city longer than any other place). The explanation is that the letter was carried by Tychicus (6:21) to Ephesus first since it was the major city in the region. From there it was circulated among the other churches.

What the Letter Looked Like

If you wrote a letter in the first century, you didn't just put it in an envelope, address it, and stick on a stamp. There was no postal system available for common people, so letters, which were written on rolls of papyrus, were tied with thread and delivered by hand. Because of this, addresses weren't necessary. Barclay writes that the titles of the New Testament letters were not part of the original papyrus versions. These were added later when the letters were collected and distributed for all the churches to read.

The phrase "God's holy people" is another way to say "saints." We tend to equate saints with great people of God who have died, but in reality a saint is anyone who has been set apart for God. You're not a saint because of anything you have done to set yourself apart from other people. You are a saint because God has set you apart so you can devote yourself to Jesus.

As "faithful followers of Christ Jesus," we have two identities. We are *human* beings with an earthly identity found in this world, and we are *spiritual* beings with a heavenly identity found in Christ Jesus. We'll talk more about this in the next chapter.

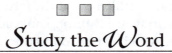

$\mathcal{S}$tudy the $\mathcal{W}$ord

1. Why do you think Paul is so careful to establish his authority as "an apostle of Christ Jesus" (1:1)?

    What's the difference between an *apostle* and a *disciple?*

    What spiritual titles in today's world carry the authority of an apostle? How do titles help or hinder your witness for Christ?

2. Read Romans 7:15-23. How do you feel about your own inner struggles after reading about Paul's conflicts?

Read Romans 7:24-25. What does Paul mean when he writes that the answer to this ongoing inner conflict is in Jesus Christ our Lord? How does this help you?

3. God established the church in order to bring all things together in Christ. The church should stand for unity. If this is the case, why is there so much divisiveness in the church?

Think of your own church. What kinds of issues tend to cause disagreement? What can you do to help maintain unity in your church?

4. Why might so many Christians be content to feed on
    the "milk" of the Word when they should be chewing
    on the "meat"?

    List three action steps you can take to further your
    journey deeper into God's Word.

5. If the Bible is God's personal message to each believer,
    what happens when you have a disagreement with
    another Christian and each of you can find scriptural
    support for your position? How do you correctly
    resolve your differences?

6. Describe your human identity in the world.

    Describe your divine identity in Christ Jesus.

Chapter 4

Spiritual and heavenly blessings are the
best blessings; with them we cannot
be miserable, and without them
we must be so.

—*Matthew Henry*

Every Spiritual Blessing

People talk a lot about self-esteem these days. If a child is having trouble in school, a common diagnosis is that he or she lacks confidence because of poor self-esteem. If an adult is having problems at home or in the workplace, others may chalk it up to low self-esteem.

If you're struggling in your Christian life, you may have low self-esteem, but it has nothing to do with you. The problem isn't that you don't think enough of yourself. The problem is that you don't think enough of God. Or at least you aren't aware of the great effort He has made to give you every spiritual blessing. This next section of Ephesians explains what God has given you and what you need to do to understand and claim these blessings.

God's Incredible Plan

Ephesians 1:3-14

The 12 verses in Ephesians 1:3-14 contain the golden nugget of Paul's entire letter. The content is amazing enough, but the way Paul delivers this section is astounding. Scholars tell us that in the Greek (the original language of the entire New Testament), these 12 verses were one long sentence. Picture Paul sitting in prison, dictating to his secretary as the Holy Spirit prompts him to describe the incredibly deep and important facts about what God has done for those who are faithful followers of Jesus. Bible scholars have compared these 12 verses to the overture of a great opera, a racehorse bursting out of the gate, and a snowball careening down a hill. Paul gushes with praise to God:

How we praise God, the Father of our Lord Jesus
Christ, who has blessed us with every spiritual
blessing in the heavenly realms because we belong
to Christ (1:3).

There's the setup for the entire book of Ephesians—
and for your Christian life. You aren't just Joe or Jane
Dokes who lives at 123 N. Main Street in Centerville. You
have been blessed with every spiritual blessing in heaven.
This isn't make-believe. It's who you are and what you
have because your identity is in Christ. You belong to the
most loving, the most personal, and the most powerful
being in the universe—and the Holy Spirit is your guarantee that this is true.

The entire Trinity is involved in this process: God the
Father, God the Son, and God the Holy Spirit. God loves
you and cares about you so much that He has given every
part of Himself to make sure you can live abundantly here
on earth and eternally in heaven. Here's how God did it...

The Father Chose Us (1:3-7)

God's decision to give us "every spiritual blessing in
the heavenly realms because we belong to Christ" wasn't
some random or recent thought. He didn't look at the
world one day and say, "I think I'll put my plan into
action now." No, God loved us and chose us "long ago,
even before he made the world" (1:4). God's nature is to
love because God is love (1 John 4:8). And because God is
eternal, He has always loved us and will always continue
to love us. So what does it mean when Paul says that God
chose us?

The Doctrine of Election (1:4)

This is a tough one for us mere mortals to understand. We like to think that we choose God, and in a sense we do. We respond to God by believing that Jesus is the answer to our sin problem (John 3:16). We ask Jesus to forgive our sins (1 John 1:9) and invite Him into our hearts (Revelation 3:20). We respond, we believe, and we invite. Isn't that choosing God? Well, from our viewpoint, yes. But from God's viewpoint, it's a much different story. In his letter to the Romans, Paul writes:

> As the Scriptures say, "No one is good—not even one. No one has real understanding; no one is seeking God. All have turned away from God; all have gone wrong. No one does good, not even one" (Romans 3:10-12).

You see, as good as we think we are, we are so sinful that we aren't capable of choosing God. We couldn't even if we tried. God must intervene in our lives and choose us to choose Him. This concept is called the doctrine of election.

What Is the Doctrine of Election All About?

The doctrine of election means that we are saved by the grace of God and not because of anything we do. Because of our sin nature, we aren't good enough to please a holy God, and we aren't capable of choosing Him either. If anything, we are God's enemies. But God, who is all-loving, all-knowing, and all-powerful, reached out to us while we were sinners (Romans 5:8). He chose—or *elected*—to save us. Not only that, but God chose us before He created the world! Long before you were born, God had a secret plan to save you, and that plan centered on Jesus Christ.

So what part do we play in all of this? Do we just sit back and wait to get elected by God? Not at all. One of the great mysteries of the Christian life is that even though God is sovereign—that is, the supreme authority—we still have a free will, and we still have to make a choice. A.W. Tozer writes: "The master choice is His, the secondary choice is ours." From God's eternal viewpoint, He must do the choosing (John 15:16). But from our limited viewpoint, we must make a choice for God by believing in Jesus (John 3:16).

The Plan of Adoption (1:5)

After God loved us and chose us, He literally and legally adopted us into His own family.

This is a very big deal. Remember, in our natural, human state we are God's enemies. We're not like the cute little puppy in the pet store window that looks at you with those sad eyes, hoping you will take him home. No, we're running from God like a distant and defiant child. But God, who is rich in love and mercy, finds us and takes us home, all because of Jesus Christ and what He did to make us friends with God (Romans 5:8-10). Because our identity is in Jesus, God adopts us into His family with all the rights and privileges that go with it.

In our world, adoption means that you legally raise someone else's child as your own. In the Roman world, the world in which Paul lived and wrote, it had even more significance. Barclay explains that under Roman law, an adopted child literally became a new person. Everything about the former family, including any debts or obligations, was eliminated as if it never existed. The adopted person then received all the rights and privileges as a legitimate member of the new family.

This is what happens to a child of God. We were once obligated to a life of sin and the consequences of that sin—death (Romans 6:23). But God adopted us out of that dead-end life into eternal life with Him. William Barclay writes: "That adoption wipes out the past and makes us new."

The Son Purchased Our Freedom (1:8-12)

Being sinners means more than just doing things that violate God's perfect standard. Being sinners means that every one of us and everything about us is thoroughly sinful. To use the metaphor of slavery, we are slaves to sin. Sin is our master (Romans 7:23). When Jesus died for our sins, He went into the slave market of sin and purchased our freedom (that's the meaning of *redemption*). And the price He paid was His own blood. Because of this act of redemption, our sins are forgiven, which makes it possible for God to adopt us into His family. Do you see how this works? You can't have God's love without Jesus' sacrifice. And you can't have Jesus' sacrifice without God's love.

The person and work of Jesus on the cross for us is at the center of God's secret plan (1:9). God has no other plan, and there is no other way in heaven or on earth to be saved, than through Jesus (John 14:6; Acts 4:12).

The Holy Spirit Is God's Guarantee (1:13-14)

So here's the truth. This is the Good News:

- God saves us.
- When we believe in Jesus, God identifies us as His own.
- God gives us His guarantee through the Holy Spirit.

The Holy Spirit has many roles in the life of the believer:

He's the Big Initiator

The Holy Spirit brings people to the point of decision about their need for salvation and God. This influence is sometimes called *conviction.* Jesus said:

> *And when he comes, he will convince the world of its sin, and of God's righteousness, and of the coming judgment* (John 16:8).

The Holy Spirit also convinces us of God's holiness, opening our eyes to see the truth about Christ's life, death, and Resurrection.

He's the Change Maker

When we respond to the Spirit's invitation, He releases His truly miraculous transforming power in our lives. We are changed—immediately and forever. Remember that "new life" we talked about in chapter 1? It's the Holy Spirit's job to give it to us.

> *But then God our Savior showed us his kindness and love. He saved us, not because of the good things we did, but because of his mercy. He washed away our sins and gave us a new life through the Holy Spirit* (Titus 3:4-5).

He's the Inside Source

The Holy Spirit comes to live inside us. His presence is very real, whether as a "still, small voice" nudging us in God's direction, or as a lifelong power to change us to be like Jesus. Paul wrote:

Don't you realize that all of you together are the temple of God and that the Spirit of God lives in you? (1 Corinthians 3:16).

He's the Family Name

The Holy Spirit "baptizes" all believers into the family of God. In this context, *baptism* means that we are given a new identity in Christ, and it has nothing to do with getting wet.

Some of us are Jews, some Gentiles, some are slaves, and some are free. But we have all been baptized into Christ's body by one Spirit, and we have all received the same Spirit (1 Corinthians 12:13).

He's the Eternal Guarantee

Another important role of the Holy Spirit is to give us the assurance that all of these things God promised will happen.

It is God who gives us, along with you, the ability to stand firm for Christ. He has commissioned us, and he has identified us as his own by placing the Holy Spirit in our hearts as the first installment of everything he will give us (2 Corinthians 1:21-22).

Remember, all of these blessings are *spiritual*. You have no material evidence for trusting in Jesus (unless you count that certificate your church gave you). These are intangible realities and promises. And since we have no physical proof these blessings exist, doubt naturally creeps in.

One of the most frequent and troubling questions nearly all new believers ask is, How do I know I'm saved? This is a very good question, and all Christians (if they are honest with themselves) ask it at one time or another. Don't be embarrassed if you've wondered about your eternal security. God anticipated your doubts and fears, and He gave you the Holy Spirit to make you feel secure from the inside out (1:13) and to guarantee that God is going to give you everything He promised (1:14).

■ ▢ ▢

Study the Word

1. Read Ephesians 1:3-14 again. List all of the spiritual blessings that this passage says are yours *from the Father*.

    List the spiritual blessings that are yours *in Jesus*.

    List the spiritual blessings that are yours *through the Holy Spirit*.

2. List three advantages of the spiritual blessings God
   has given us over the material ones.

3. Why is it so difficult for people to understand and
   accept the doctrine of election?

What is your honest reaction to Ephesians 1:4-5?

Read Mark 16:15-16. How do you reconcile the doctrine of election with the Great Commission?

4. What does Paul mean when he says this about God's secret plan: "At the right time he will bring everything together under the authority of Christ—everything in heaven and on earth" (1:10)?

5. Explain in a paragraph what being chosen and adopted by God means.

6. Christianity has been called an "exclusive" religion, and Christians have been accused of being "intolerant." In what ways is Christianity exclusive, and in what ways is it inclusive? Support your answers with Scripture.

In what ways should a Christian be intolerant, and in what ways should a Christian be tolerant? Support your answers with Scripture.

7. Why does the church experience so much misunderstanding about the Holy Spirit? Did you have any misconceptions this chapter addressed?

Based on what you have read and learned from Ephesians 1:3-14, reflect on what God has done for you, beginning in eternity past and continuing into eternity future. How might this knowledge change the way you live the Christian life here and now?

Chapter 5

When a person chokes or drowns and stops breathing, there is nothing he can do. If he ever breathes again it will be because someone else starts him breathing. A person who is spiritually dead cannot even make a decision of faith unless God first breathes into him the breath of spiritual life. Faith is simply breathing the breath that God's grace supplies.

—*John MacArthur*

Flooded with Light

In the first part of Ephesians, Paul gushes with praise to God, who has blessed us with every spiritual blessing (1:3), who has poured out His wonderful kindness on us because we belong to Jesus (1:6), and who has guaranteed everything through the Holy Spirit (1:14). Now, in Ephesians 1:15-18, Paul pauses, pulls up a chair, looks us square in the eye and says, "Beloved, do you realize what you have here? Do you understand what it means to be blessed by God in such an extravagant manner?" Paul prays that our hearts will be "flooded with light" so we will understand what God has done by adopting us and identifying with us.

Like Paul, we pray that you will understand just how much God has done for you and just how much you need God. We hope this chapter will help you grow in your understanding and appreciation of how much God loves you and how amazing His grace really is.

God's Amazing Grace

Ephesians 1:15–2:10

*W*hat's *A*head

- ☐ Understanding How Powerful God Is (1:19-23)

- ☐ Understanding How Powerless We Were (2:1-10)

*M*any Christians don't realize what God has done for them, and this comes across in two different ways. First, you have the "Tim the Tool Man" Christians, who are constantly asking God for more. "O Lord, give us your power," they pray. "We need your blessings." Then there are the complacent Christians, who figure they don't need anything else from God, and they don't need to know anything else about God. They live by the motto: "God said it, I believe it, that settles it for me."

To both of these kinds of Christians, Paul says, "Wake up and smell the coffee!" You don't need more power. You are already plugged into the God of the universe, the greatest power source of all. But don't just sit there like it doesn't matter. You need to act on what you already have.

Paul's desire and his constant prayer is that his fellow believers would know God better by fully understanding two things: how powerful God is and how powerless we were before God saved us.

Growing in the Knowledge of God

The key to growing in the Christian life is to grow in the knowledge of God. We need to pray, as Paul did, for God to give us "spiritual wisdom and understanding" so we can grow in our knowledge of God (1:17). Barclay explains that *wisdom* is intellectual knowledge. We need to know the truth about God in detail, and that requires study. *Understanding* is more like practical knowledge that helps us to handle the day-to-day problems of life, and that means we have to put into practice what we know.

In other words, you need both "book smarts" and "street smarts" when it comes to knowing God. You need to engage your whole person—your mind as well as your emotions—as you get to know God better. Only then will you be able to fully appreciate your "wonderful future" and your "glorious inheritance" (1:18).

Understand How Powerful God Is (1:19-23)

Of all the things we need to know about God, knowing how incredibly powerful He is is one of the most important because God's power is available to us. And just what kind of power are we talking about? The Greek word for *power* here is *dunamis* (it's where we get the word *dynamite*). This is miraculous, abundant, dynamite power! And this power doesn't just sit on the shelf. This power is "for us who believe him." Literally, God's power energizes us. To amplify his point about power, Paul tells us what this power is capable of doing:

Power over Death (1:20)

John Stott writes that "death is a bitter and relentless enemy." All of us will face death someday (Hebrews 9:27). But God's power can defeat death, and He proved it by raising Jesus Christ from the dead.

Power over Evil (1:21)

God didn't raise Jesus from the dead just so He could keep living on earth. God raised Jesus and seated Him "in the place of honor at God's right hand in the heavenly realms" (1:20). In this place Jesus rules with power over "any ruler or authority or power or leader or anything else in this world or in the world to come" (1:21). God's power is more powerful than anything this evil world has to offer.

Power over the Church (1:22-23)

Jesus is the head of the church, which is His body. We talk about "going to church," but that's not really the church at all—at least not the way Paul describes it. The church is the body of Christ, and because we belong to Christ, we are the church, filled with the presence and power of God.

Comprehending God's incredible power is one thing; experiencing it is quite another. How many times do you feel weak rather than powerful? How often are you frustrated because your weaknesses—such as deceit, lust, greed, jealousy, and pride—seem to displace God's power in your life? This tension can be a problem, but only if you believe that your weaknesses are beyond God's power. God understands where you have come from (and Paul is going to tell you in the next section). God knows that you still struggle with sin. That's why He has given you His power—to work within you to accomplish infinitely more than you could ever imagine (3:20).

Understand How Powerless We Were (2:1-10)

We tend to have a pretty inflated view of ourselves, especially regarding spiritual matters. Many people believe that God saves us because we're basically good folks. Even some Christians buy into this idea. In the first three verses of Ephesians 2, Paul tells us exactly who we were and where we came from before God saved us. Paul isn't twisting our arm until we say, "Okay, we get it; we're wretched, miserable human beings!" He simply wants us to put ourselves in perspective. We need to understand who we were without Christ and who we are with Christ.

Life Without Christ (2:1-3)

Ephesians 2:1-3 contains the clearest and most concise description of the natural human condition in the entire Bible. Paul highlights three characteristics, and they aren't pretty:

- We were *dead* and doomed forever because of our sin natures.

- We were *enslaved* to sin and to Satan, following him rather than God.

- We were *under God's anger.*

This is who we were in our natural state. Because of our sin nature, we were enemies of a holy God. We were under God's anger, not because He is against us but because of God's complete and total opposition to sin and evil. Truly, we were in a sorry and desperate state.

Life with Christ (2:4-10)

The first word in Ephesians 2:4 isn't very glamorous, but it's one of the sweetest words Paul could have used. The word is *But*. It's the word that sets up the next section. It's the word that tells us we are no longer dead, enslaved, and under God's anger. It's the word that gives us hope. Despite all we are and the desperate condition we are in, God has not given up on us. God, who is rich in mercy, extravagant in love, and abundant in grace, has raised us from spiritual death just as surely as He raised Christ from the dead. In fact, we have life because of the Resurrection of Jesus Christ.

This section of Ephesians is one of the most significant in all of Scripture because it's all about our salvation from death to life. In three powerful verses, Paul explains how and why God saved us.

God saved you by His special favor when you believed (2:8).

Memorize this verse. It tells you *how* God saved you: by His *grace*. The definition of grace is *special favor*. It means getting something we don't deserve. Along with His grace, God gives us His *mercy,* which means He doesn't give us the penalty we deserve because of our sins, and that penalty is death. So, not only does God not punish us for what we deserve, but He also gives us the salvation we don't deserve.

Our salvation is a gift that God gives us out of His extravagant love. We can't earn God's special favor and we can't take credit for it. Our salvation has been accomplished *with* Christ (2:6), *through* Christ (2:7), and *in* Christ Jesus (2:10). We can find special favor with God only because of who Jesus Christ is and what He has done. Our job is to trust that what God accomplished with, through, and in Christ is all we need to be saved.

This is where *faith* comes in. The only way to receive God's gift of salvation is to believe that what Christ accomplished for us is the only way to escape our death penalty and inherit eternal life. And even faith isn't something that we can manufacture on our own. Even the ability to believe in Jesus is a gift from God.

Salvation is not a reward for the good things we have done (2:9).

Every other religion, cult, and spiritual belief in the world teaches that salvation depends on the good things we do, commonly referred to as "works." Christianity alone teaches that we can do nothing to earn our salvation. Nothing good lived in us (remember, we were dead because of sin), and no amount of good we can do would ever meet God's perfect standard (see Romans 3:23). The only reason God has declared us "not guilty" is because Jesus died to take away our sins (Romans 3:24). We're not good enough to satisfy God's anger against us, but Jesus is (Romans 3:25).

We are God's masterpiece (2:10).

Christians occasionally have a tendency to take this grace business too far. The way we sometimes figure it, since there's nothing we can do to earn God's salvation, there's nothing we can do to take it away. So we live a life "under grace," pretty much doing what we want to do. Admittedly, we can do nothing to earn salvation, but that doesn't mean we have nothing to do. To the contrary, God saved us through Jesus "so that we can do the good things he planned for us long ago" (2:10). William Barclay calls this the "Pauline Paradox." We are not saved *because* of good works, but God "created us anew in Christ Jesus" so we could do good works. God's grace is the *means* of salvation, but good works are the *evidence* of salvation.

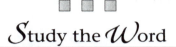

$\mathcal{S}$tudy the $\mathcal{W}$ord

1. Are you a "Tim the Tool Man" Christian or a complacent Christian? Be honest. What can you do to fully realize and utilize God's power in your life? (See Ephesians 1:15-23.)

2. Why do you need both "book smarts" and "street smarts" to know God and grow as a Christian? Make a list of the things you are doing to get smarter in each category.

   Book smarts:

   Street smarts:

3. Describe two experiences in your own life when God's power energized you. For one example, think of a time when God gave you power in your struggle over sin. For the other example, recall a time when God gave you power to accomplish more than you ever thought you could.

4. Read Ephesians 2:1-3. What situations or circumstances in the world today demonstrate the truth of these verses?

    Is God to blame for being angry with the people He created? Why or why not?

5. What might be the reason that God has gone to so much trouble to save us? Why didn't God simply wipe out the world and start over (see Genesis 6:5-8)?

6. John Stott writes that Ephesians 2:8 contains the "three foundation words of the good news—salvation, grace, and faith." In what way is each of these elements essential to God's plan to save us with, through, and in Christ Jesus (see Ephesians 1:9-13)?

Salvation:

Grace:

Faith:

7. Read Ephesians 2:10. What good things do you think God has prepared for you to do in the short term?

In the long term?

Are you on a path (career, ministry, family, etc.) that is preparing you to do good things? If God planned good things for us to do long ago, what do we need to do to prepare ourselves?

Chapter 6

Christ is both peace and peacemaker. He actually brought about the reconciliation of Jew and Gentile when he died on the cross. Then he made both into one.

—*A. Skevington Wood*

He Broke Down the Wall

Throughout history, groups of people have been hostile toward one another. In our time, we are painfully aware of the sometimes deadly conflicts between Muslims and Jews. Our headlines have also informed us of the hatred between the Catholics and the Protestants in Ireland, as well as the Croats and the Serbs in Bosnia. In this next section of Ephesians, Paul writes about the hostility that once existed between Jews and Gentiles. In fact, all humanity was hostile to God.

We can thank God that He didn't leave us in this hostile condition. He arranged for permanent peace treaties between Jews and Gentiles and between Himself and humanity. He broke down the wall, and He did it through the Prince of Peace, Jesus Christ.

God's Wonderful Peace

Ephesians 2:11-22

*I*n chapter 3 we gave you the central message of Ephesians:

> Without Christ, this world can only experience disunity. God's plan is to unite all things in Christ.

In this section Paul builds a case for why we need this unity and explains how God will accomplish it through Christ. First, he reminds the Gentile believers in Ephesus of who they once were—without God and without hope.

Helpless and Hopeless (2:11-12)

Before we explain why the Gentiles were helpless and hopeless, we need to look at the differences between Jews and Gentiles.

A *Jew* is a Hebrew, a descendent of Abraham (Genesis 12:23). God promised Abraham that his descendants would be a great nation (not a nation in the traditional sense with borders and such, but a nation of people). God also promised to bless His chosen people and to bless the world through them. Theologians agree that this "blessing" came through the person of Jesus Christ, who came to the nation of Israel as the promised Messiah (Isaiah 53).

A *Gentile* is basically anyone who isn't a Jew. Pious Jews—"the circumcised ones"—called the Gentiles "outsiders by birth." Jews had great contempt for Gentiles. If a Jew married a Gentile, a funeral was held for the Jew because such contact with a Gentile was the same as death.

Compared to the Jews, Paul writes, the Gentiles had three disadvantages (2:12):

- They were **living apart from Christ**. They had no prospects of a Messiah to save them.

- They were **excluded from God's people.** They could not share in the spiritual blessings promised to God's chosen people.

- They were **without God and without hope.** The Gentiles had many gods, but they didn't have the one true God of Israel. And because they were without God, they had no hope.

The outlook was bleak. The Gentiles were "far away from God." If God had not intervened, the "wall of hostility" between Jews and Gentiles would have remained.

Breaking Down the Wall (2:13-18)

When Paul wrote about a "wall of hostility" between Jews and Gentiles, he wasn't just using figurative language. William Barclay writes that there was a literal wall in the Jewish Temple that prevented Gentiles from entering the innermost courts. Gentiles could walk into an outer court (called the Court of the Gentiles), but any Gentile who ventured past the wall and into an inner court was in danger of being put to death instantly. Paul knew from personal experience what this wall of hostility was all about. In chapter 2 we explained that after Paul left Ephesus, he went to Corinth and then Jerusalem, where a riot broke out and Paul was almost killed. The incident that infuriated the Jews was a false rumor that Paul had brought an Ephesian Gentile by the name of Trophimus into the Temple past the wall (Acts 21:28-29). The "wall of hostility" between Jews and Gentiles almost cost Paul his life.

Walls of Hostility Then and Now

We may think those kinds of walls existed only in the ancient world, but they are just as prevalent in our world today. Walls and fences separate some nations and are usually guarded by armed troops. Walls and fences separate and isolate some neighbors from each other. Racial barriers create hostility between people. As Barclay writes: "Modern progress has made the world a neighborhood; God has given us the task of making it a brotherhood."

There is only one way to break down the wall of hostility between Jews and Gentiles or between any other groups. There is only one solution to the enduring conflict in our world. His name is Jesus, the Prince of Peace. Jesus came to earth for one purpose, and that was to die for our sins in order to break down the walls that separate us from each other and from God. In this section of Ephesians we learn that several things were accomplished by the death of Jesus:

- Jesus broke down the wall of hostility and made peace between Jews and Gentiles by making us one people (2:14).

- Jesus created one new body from the two groups (2:15).

- Jesus put to death the hostility between Jews and Gentiles, and He made peace between both groups and God (2:16).

- Jesus brought the Good News of peace to everyone (2:17).

- Jesus made a way for all people to come to God the Father through the Holy Spirit (2:18).

As we're going to find out, this is God's secret plan for one people. God has brought unity and peace to the world "because of what Christ has done for us." Of course, not everyone enjoys this peace, and the world is still a place of conflict and will remain that way until Jesus returns to earth a second time to end all conflict once and for all and bring everlasting peace. Meanwhile, Barclay explains what it means to have unity in Christ:

> The unity in Christ produces Christians whose Christianity transcends all their local and racial differences; it produces men who are friends

with each other because they are friends with
God; it produces men who are one because they
meet in the presence of God to whom they all
have access.

Citizens of a New Family (2:19-22)

God brought unity to two groups previously divided,
but He didn't stop there. God also created a new family—
the family of God—that includes all people who have
been brought together in Christ. This is that new identity
we have been talking about. We are no longer "strangers
and foreigners." We are members of God's family. We are
citizens of a new group of people known as the church.

True Citizenship

Anyone who lives in a foreign country without citizenship is
considered an alien. You're like a stranger in a strange land.
That's the way we once were with God. Our sin disqualified us
from citizenship in God's eternal kingdom. But because of what
Christ has done for us, we have become "citizens along with all
of God's holy people." Together with all people who believe in
the person and work of Christ for salvation, we are members of
God's family.

Paul closes this chapter by using the analogy of a great
house. Together, all who believe in Jesus are the house,
"built on the foundation of the apostles and the
prophets." God has fitted us together like stones to create
a holy temple for His glory. The most important stone,
of course, is the cornerstone, and that is Christ. This is a
true picture of the church:

Through him you Gentiles are also joined together as part of this dwelling where God lives by his Spirit (2:22).

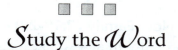

Study the Word

1. Read John 1:1-14. Who is the "Word"?

    What does John mean when he writes: "Even in his own land and among his own people, he was not accepted"? Who are "his own people"?

    What does "all who believed in him and accepted him" mean?

2. Compare John 1:1-14 with Ephesians 2:11-13.

Have the Gentiles ever rejected Christ in the same way that "his own people" did?

3. Read Genesis 12:3. Who are "all the families of the earth"? How are they blessed through Abraham?

4. List three ways that Jesus Christ qualifies as the greatest reconciler of all time.

5. In Ephesians 2:15 Paul writes: "By his death he ended the whole system of Jewish law that excluded the Gentiles. His purpose was to make peace between Jews and Gentiles by creating in himself one new person from the two groups."

   In what sense did Christ end the law?

   Who is the "one new person"?

6. Read 2 Corinthians 5:17-21. What can you do to rec-
    oncile people to Jesus?

7. Are there any "walls of hostility" that exist between
    you and another person or group of people? What
    can you do to break these walls down?

Chapter 7

For thousands of years God kept a secret in his heart, hidden from the world, from the angels, from the priests, from the patriarchs, and from the prophets until the time came for him to reveal it through his Son to his holy apostles.

—*Max Anders*

Special Assignment

Don't you love movies about secret agents? Whether it's cool Mr. Phelps and his Mission Impossible Force, the unflappable James Bond, or the goofy Austin Powers, it's fun to imagine yourself as a daring spy who lives with secrets and a double identity.

Well, if you're a Christian who wants to live your life full out for God, you don't have to imagine being a secret agent at all. You already are one! You're like an undercover agent who has been given a secret identity and a special assignment from God.

In the first two chapters of Ephesians, you have discovered your secret identity in Christ. Now, beginning in Ephesians 3, you are going to get your secret mission. Read on!

God's Purpose in the Body

Ephesians 3:1-21

*S*ometimes secret agents get into tight spots, and Paul was no exception. As we learned in chapter 2, Paul wrote his letter to the church at Ephesus while he was in prison. He begins this section of his letter by reminding the Ephesians that he is "a prisoner of Christ Jesus" because of his preaching to "you Gentiles." Paul was actually in a Roman prison (courtesy of Emperor Nero), but he considered himself a prisoner of Jesus.

Was Paul confused? Was he blaming heaven for his earthly imprisonment? Not at all. Paul was honored to be doing time for the sake of Jesus. He had the proper perspective. Paul may have had an earthly identity as a Roman citizen, but he lived his life with the knowledge of his secret identity as a citizen of heaven. And he felt privileged to be chosen to "explain to everyone this plan that God, the Creator of all things, had kept secret from the beginning" (3:9).

God's Secret Plan (3:1-13)

So what is this mystery that Paul is so excited about? What is God's secret plan? It's really simple but very big. God's secret plan involves the body of Christ, or the church.

> *And this is the secret plan: The Gentiles have an equal share with the Jews in all the riches inherited by God's children. Both groups have believed the Good News, and both are part of the same body and enjoy together the promise of blessings through Christ Jesus* (3:6).

We cannot overstate the importance of this announcement to the world. Previous generations didn't know this Good News because God did not reveal it to them (3:5). But now the Christians in Asia Minor and everyone since then knows that salvation by grace—not by works—is available to anyone who believes that Jesus is the way, the truth, and the life, and that nobody can come to God except through Him (John 14:6).

Because of Christ, both Jews and Gentiles "are part of the same body and enjoy together the promise of blessings through Christ Jesus." This is the eternal purpose of God. It is no longer a future event. The body of Christ—the church—made up of believing Jews and Gentiles, is something for now. The church is God's showcase. It's His crowning achievement.

God was so proud of His plan to bring people together into one body in Christ that He announced it to "all the rulers and authorities in the heavenly realms" (3:10). Talk about an effective marketing campaign! Even the angels didn't know about God's secret plan, but now they do, and it's thrilling for them. John Stott writes about the angels: "We are to think of them as spectators of the drama of salvation." Jesus explained what happens when someone accepts God's free gift of salvation:

> *In the same way, there is joy in the presence of God's angels when even one sinner repents* (Luke 15:10).

Think of it! When you believed in Jesus by faith, the angels of heaven rejoiced.

Good Angels and Bad Angels

The angels who rejoiced when you came to Christ are "good" angels. That is to say, they were not among the angels who followed Satan in rebellion against God (Isaiah 14:12-14). The "bad" angels, also known as demons, were also aware of your conversion, but they didn't do any rejoicing. Paul gives advice on how to stand up to these "evil rulers and authorities" in Ephesians 6, and we'll discuss that with you in chapter 13.

Fall on Your Knees (3:14-19)

We hope you are beginning to understand the implications of this incredible truth. It was such a startling revelation to Paul that he fell to his knees in awe and offered a prayer to God. This should be our response as we gradually realize just how much God has done for us by saving us through Christ. We say "gradually" because these lofty truths don't come overnight. And we can't learn them simply by using our rational thought. We must invite the Holy Spirit to guide our thoughts and allow Him to penetrate our hearts so that we can appreciate what God has done and incorporate what we know into our lives. Paul wrote to the Corinthian church:

> *But we know these things because God has revealed them to us by his Spirit, and his Spirit searches out everything and shows us even God's deep secrets* (1 Corinthians 2:10).

That is what Paul is praying for here in Ephesians: that the Holy Spirit would illuminate our hearts and our thinking so we would know these deep and mysterious secrets of God. Let's look at Paul's prayer in detail. He prays for four things. Each of these elements builds on the previous one. Stott calls it a "prayer-staircase."

1. Paul prays that we would be strengthened on the inside by the Holy Spirit (3:16).

Paul is not praying for us to have more of the Holy Spirit, but for us to understand the inner strength we already have. As a Christian, you already have all of the Holy Spirit you're ever going to get (that's all of Him, by the way). But the Spirit can't do His work unless you give Him a willing heart to work with.

2. Paul prays that Christ will be more at home in our hearts (3:17).

When we let the Holy Spirit do His work in our hearts, Christ will be more "at home." Think of your life as a house with various rooms and doors. Christ might live in your house but not be "at home." This happens when you keep certain rooms "closed off" to the Holy Spirit. Later in Ephesians, Paul talks about letting the Holy Spirit fill and control you (5:18). He needs to have the full run of your house. No rooms are closed, nothing is held back. When this happens, Jesus can be at home in your house and your heart.

3. Paul prays that our roots would go deep into the soil of God's love (3:17-18).

When we give the Holy Spirit the run of our house and Jesus settles in, we can begin to experience God's marvelous love. Love is the essence of God. When we experience God's love, we experience God. Paul goes on to pray that we would have the power to understand the full dimension of God's love:

- *How wide*—God's love is broad enough to cover all our experiences.

- *How long*—God's love lasts every day of our lives and throughout eternity.

- *How high*—Nothing in heaven can compete with God's love.

- *How deep*—Nothing on earth or below earth can overshadow God's love.

4. Paul prays that we would live life to the fullest and be filled with God's power (3:19).

When we give the Holy Spirit the run of our house and Jesus settles in, and we begin to experience God's multi-dimensional love, we will begin to live the abundant Christian life everyone talks about but so few Christians seem to have. To be filled with God's fullness is to experience God fully. Of course, we can never have all of God or know Him completely in this life, but we can enjoy all the power God has to offer us now—if we take these steps Paul prays for.

This is rarefied air! If Paul's prayer is like a staircase, it's a high one. "Climbers of this staircase become short of breath, even a little giddy," writes Stott. Reaching the top step is like reaching the top of Mount Everest. This should be the constant goal of every Christian.

Three Steps Up, Two Steps Down

You won't stay on top of the staircase all the time, regardless of how badly you want to be there. Lack of faith, too much worry, and just plain old sin can quickly knock you down a step or two. Don't get discouraged! If you lack faith, ask God to help you. If you worry too much, give your cares to God (1 Peter 5:7). When you sin, ask God to forgive you (1 John 1:9). Then begin climbing the staircase again.

To God Be the Glory (3:20-21)

Paul concludes his prayer with a *doxology* or hymn of praise to God. He thanks God and gives Him the glory for all that He has done for us in Christ and for all that He continues to do. When God works His power in and through the lives of top-step Christians, He does things that we wouldn't even dare to ask for or dream about. God doesn't merely meet our expectations. He delights in blowing our minds, not because we are so great but because Jesus is so great. We can never take credit for the awesome things God does in our lives, but we can thank Him and give Him glory "in the church and in Christ Jesus."

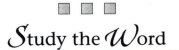

Study the Word

1. Even though Paul was in prison and Nero was his emperor, he placed his confidence in the sovereignty of God. Are you experiencing any difficult circumstances that seem to be under someone else's control? In what way might God be working behind the scenes in your situation? What statement of faith can you make to declare your trust in God? (See Hebrews 2:10.)

2. God didn't tell "previous generations" about His secret plan to bring believers together into the body of Christ (3:5). Without this Good News (3:7), how were people in previous generations saved? (See Romans 4:1-5.)

3. Paul writes that God revealed his "plan regarding Christ...by the Holy Spirit to his holy apostles and prophets" (3:4-5). How is God's plan passed on to people today?

   What part can you play in passing on the plan?

   Who is responsible to spread this Good News? Use Scripture to support your answer.

4. Why does God need to "show his wisdom in all its rich variety to all the rulers and authorities in the heavenly realms"?

5. Reflect on Paul's "prayer-staircase" (Ephesians 3:16-19). Why might the stairs be in this order?

   - Inner strength through the Holy Spirit

   - Christ at home in your heart

   - Roots deep in the soil of God's love

   - Filled with God's power

6. Mountain climbers train extensively to scale the world's highest mountains, and they don't attempt their climbs without special equipment. What kind of training can you do to scale God's prayer-staircase?

   What kind of special equipment do you have to assist you?

7. Do you really believe that God is able to accomplish "infinitely more than we would ever dare to ask or hope"? If so, what incredible things do you think God wants to accomplish in your life? Dream big!

Chapter 8

The Christian idea is not that of a number
of "integrated" individuals, concerned
about their own spiritual progress, but of
growth into Christ, as members of the
Body of Christ, in which we all live
by the same Life, which flows through
the Body, and animates us all.

—*Olive Wyon*

Worthy of Your Calling

There's an old story about the world conqueror Alexander the Great. The mythic Macedonian was inspecting his troops when he came upon a shabbily dressed soldier. "What's your name?" the great military genius asked. "Alexander," the soldier replied. Without missing a beat, Alexander the Commander took a step forward and said to the now-trembling infantryman, "Either change your ways or change your name."

There's a lesson in that story for those of us who call ourselves "Christian." Are we shabby spiritual soldiers who are an embarrassment to our Commander in Chief? Or do we possess the characteristics that tell the world we belong to Christ?

As the second half of Ephesians begins, Paul begs us to live up to the great name we have been given. "Lead a life worthy of your calling, for you have been called by God."

Unity in the Body

Ephesians 4:1-16

*P*aul's letter to the Christians in Ephesus and beyond is now half over. So far, Paul has focused on your identity in Christ. He has told you the grand and eternal purpose of God to create a new society of believers called the church. Now, beginning with Ephesians 4, the second half of the letter shifts from what God has done for you to what you can do for God. The first half of Ephesians contained the *ingredients of belief* and focused on God. The second half will contain the *instructions for behavior* and focuses on you.

This is only fair, because even though God sees you for who you are, the world sees you for what you do. God is glorified through the behavior of His people as they are filled by the Holy Spirit, motivated by the love of Jesus, and empowered by God.

Live Up to the Family Name (4:1-2)

The opening word in Ephesians 4, "therefore," connects the next idea to everything Paul has said in the first three chapters. He's saying, "Because of everything God has done for you, I beg you to lead a life worthy of your calling." In other words, live up to the family name. Paul lists four qualities in Ephesians 4:2 that characterize people who follow Christ.

- *Humility*—Humble people aren't wimps. Even though society may consider humility to be a sign of weakness, it actually shows strength of character. Humility means having the proper perspective and the correct attitude before God. Humility keeps us God-centered rather than self-centered. Humility regards the needs of others as more important than our own needs.

- *Gentleness*—Whereas humility is an attitude, gentleness involves action. The word *gentleness* literally means "power under control." For power to be effective, it must be restrained. As God gives us His power, we need to use it to love others by springing into action with humility.

- *Patience*—In a nutshell, patience means waiting. When you are characterized by patience, you are willing to wait on the Lord for His timing. You are willing to wait for other people whose personalities annoy you. And you are willing to wait for God's answer when you are experiencing difficulties.

- *Making allowance for each other's faults because of your love*—The emphasis here is on forgiveness, on putting up with other people even if they put you off. The kind of love that makes allowance for the faults of others is unselfish *agape* love.

Work for Team Unity (4:3-6)

If we live our lives with these characteristics, then we will clearly be "united in the Holy Spirit" (4:3). We will be on the same team—God's team. In sports, nothing is more frustrating than a team of talented players who don't get along. They bicker, fight, make excuses, and blame each other. Teams without unity don't win championships. On the other hand, a team of average players can win because of their unity and team spirit. Paul makes a case for Christians to work together by staying united in the Holy Spirit. And the way to do that is to focus on the essential elements of spiritual unity (4:4-6).

- *One body*—Jesus Christ is the only way to God, and His body is the only church. There may be many denominations and church buildings, but all believers are united in one universal body, the church.

- *One Spirit*—You hear a lot of talk about "spirit" these days, but don't be fooled by hollow imitations. There is only one Holy Spirit, who unites all believers and guides them into the truth about God.

- *One glorious future*—This is the hope that we have: When we die, we will be resurrected to eternal life.

- **One Lord**—There is only one name that people may call on to save them, and that is *Jesus*. He is God's only Son, and He is the one Savior. Jesus gives us our one identity.

- **One faith**— Jesus Christ is the object of our one faith. This is the only faith that saves us. No other faith and no other object of faith will do.

- **One baptism**—To be baptized means to be identified with. There is only one baptism that identifies us with Christ, and that's the baptism into one body by the Holy Spirit.

- **One God and Father**—A crucial part of the Christian faith is this: There is one God, and above Him is no other. The first commandment says, "Do not worship any other gods besides me" (Exodus 20:3). God is singular. He is the one and only.

Enjoy Diversity (4:7-12)

Even though we are unified as believers by all of these elements, we maintain our individuality. In fact, God has designed the body to include and even encourage diversity. Christians are not mindless robots who sacrifice their gifts and personalities for a "one size fits all" faith. God has "given each one of us a special gift according to the generosity of Christ" (4:7).

Out of His generosity, Jesus gave these gifts to the church:

- **Apostles**—In the strictest sense, apostles were chosen by Jesus and saw Him after the Resurrection. In a more general sense, apostles are "sent ones." In this context the gift of apostle is used to describe those people in the early church who were sent out as representatives of the church. Most scholars believe that the gift of apostle disappeared as the early apostles died out.

Ascending and Descending

Sometimes you run into a passage of Scripture that at first glance doesn't seem to fit. But when you take a closer look, you understand the reason why it's there. Here in Ephesians 4 there is a parenthetical statement showing us that Jesus has made it possible for us to have spiritual gifts because He ascended into heaven (4:8-10). We serve a living Christ who sits at the Father's right hand as our Advocate (Hebrews 9:24). Now, if Christ ascended, then He first "came down to the lowly world in which we live" (4:9). This refers to the Incarnation, which means God became a human in the person of Jesus so He could live on earth and die for our sins. Jesus has experienced all of life and death. He has lived on earth and He lives in heaven. Jesus fills the entire universe (4:10), and He fills the body of believers with His love and His gifts.

- *Prophets*—Although they were specially gifted, prophets in the early church were different than those who had the gift of prophecy (1 Corinthians 12:10). Sometimes these prophets would foretell the future (Acts 11:28), but more often they would encourage the believers (Acts 15:32).

- *Evangelists*—These were the traveling missionaries who would go out and proclaim the Good News (that's what *evangelizing* means). They were also church planters who would lead people to Christ and then instruct them in the basics of God's Word before moving on to another location. A missionary today functions as an evangelist.

- ***Pastors and teachers***—These aren't different people, but rather two aspects of one gift. Whereas evangelists traveled from place to place, pastor-teachers served the local church by leading the people and teaching the Word of God just as they do today.

The main reason why Christ gave these gifts to His church is found in Ephesians 4:12: "Their responsibility is to equip God's people to do his work and build up the church, the body of Christ." One of the big problems in the church today is that people look to their spiritual leaders to do the work of ministry. Jesus did not intend the church to work that way. In a very real sense, everyone in the church is a minister, but not everyone is a pastor. You may not have a title or a theological degree, but you have been entrusted by Jesus to do His work and to build up the church. Your pastors and church leaders are responsible to equip and encourage you to discover and develop your spiritual gifts; you are responsible to use those gifts in the work of serving God as you serve others.

What About the Other Gifts?

You might be wondering about the other spiritual gifts, such as teaching, service, administration, etc. Why aren't they listed here? The four gifts in Ephesians 4:11 are the foundational gifts. In other words, the church was founded on the work of apostles, prophets, and evangelists, and then it was built up to maturity through the leadership of pastor-teachers. The Bible describes more than 15 different types of gifts (see 1 Corinthians 12:28-31 and Romans 12:6-8 for more listings), all of which are meant to equip believers to serve others and share the Good News of the Gospel.

Grow to Maturity (4:13-16)

There's no question that doing ministry takes work (that's why we call it the "work of ministry"), but it's not like you're working without purpose. In addition to the joy of seeing other people come to Christ and grow in their faith, you will receive another astounding benefit. You will become more like Christ! Shouldn't that be the goal of every believer? We should want to become "mature and full grown in the Lord, measuring up to the full stature of Christ" (4:13). Nothing is wrong with being a baby Christian when you first get saved. You're kind of cute. But if you're still spiritually helpless after a few years, expecting others to feed and change you, you're not very cute anymore.

Here are some other benefits to Christian maturity:

You won't be susceptible to false teaching (4:14).

Immature Christians are sometimes easily swayed by ideas that are contrary to the Bible. They don't know the ideas are wrong because they don't know the Bible. A mature believer knows the difference between heresy (false teaching) and truth.

You will strike a balance between the truth and love (4:15).

Mature Christians don't use truth like a hammer, pounding anyone who disagrees with them. We need to know and defend God's truth as revealed in Scripture, but we need to learn to tell the difference between the essentials (such as the centrality of Christ) and the non-essentials (such as the style of music in church). We shouldn't fight over nonessential issues. On the other hand, we shouldn't sacrifice the essential truths about God on the altar of love and unity.

You will help others grow into healthy, mature members of the body of Christ (4:16).

Too often the emphasis in churches today is to grow by adding numbers. This kind of growth is fine, but even more important is the growth of individuals into mature members of the body. As you mature spiritually, one of your greatest rewards will be to help others do the same.

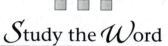

Study the Word

1. Why are the *ingredients of belief* and the *instructions for behavior* both required for us to successfully live the Christian life?

    Why might Paul have written his *ingredients of belief* before his *instructions for behavior?*

2. Are you facing a situation that challenges you to grow in one of the character traits listed in Ephesians 4:1-2: humility, gentleness, patience, or making allowance for the faults of others?

Compare this list of Christian characteristics with the fruit of the Spirit Paul lists in Galatians 5:22-23.

3. Read Ephesians 4:4-6 and review the essential elements of spiritual unity. How do these seven "ones" lead to unity among believers everywhere?

4. Why do you think God places such a strong emphasis on unity? Why do people in general and Christians in particular have so much trouble staying unified?

List three benefits to unity.

5. In His wisdom, Christ gave you at least one spiritual gift. Do you know what it is? How can you use your gift to do God's work and build up the church? If you don't know what gift or gifts God has given you, how can you discover them? (See 1 Corinthians 12:4-11 and Romans 12:6-8.)

6. Read Ephesians 4:12-13. What does Paul mean when he describes mature believers as "full grown in the Lord, measuring up to the full stature of Christ"?

   What do immature believers contribute to the body of Christ?

7. Read Ephesians 4:14-16. What would a community of believers who have these characteristics look like? How would these characteristics make your church different than it is now? How about your family? Your city?

*C*hapter 9

The more we appropriate God into our lives
the more progress we make on the road of
Christian godliness and holiness.

—*Madame Jeanne Guyon*

$\mathcal{T}$he $\mathcal{W}$ay of the $\mathcal{G}$odly

As citizens of earth, we live in a dark culture. Oh, we may be enlightened in some areas, such as science and technology, but we experience an overall darkness that comes from the sin that inhabits each person on earth, as well as from "the evil rulers and authorities of the unseen world" (6:12). As a Christian, you have another citizenship—a secret identity in Christ—that requires you to live differently from your fellow earthly citizens. But just because you are a Christian doesn't mean that you will automatically live the way God wants you to. You have to make a choice between two ways of living. You can choose to live the way you used to live, which is the way of the ungodly, or you can choose to live the way Christ wants you to live, which is the way of the godly.

In this chapter we are going to look at Paul's call to godly living, which is the way God wants us to live in the body.

Living in the Body

Ephesians 4:17-32

*W*hen God saved you by His grace, you became a new person. Paul wrote to the Corinthians:

What this means is that those who become Christians become new persons. They are not the same anymore, for the old life is gone. A new life has begun! (2 Corinthians 5:17).

As far as God is concerned, your old life is gone. Because of what Christ did for you on the cross, God sees you as a righteous person. However, this has to do with your *position* in Christ. Your everyday *experience* is an entirely different matter. As a Christian, you have a new spiritual nature. But you still have your old sin nature to deal with. Positionally, you are no longer a slave to sin

(Romans 6:6). But experientially, you are still capable of letting sin control the way you live (Romans 6:12).

In a very real sense, you have a choice to live one of two different ways. You can revert to your natural life, where sin is your master, or you can aspire to your supernatural life, where Jesus is your master. You live in a sinful world, but that's no excuse to follow the ways of the world. You have a responsibility to follow the ways of Christ.

The Way the Ungodly Live (4:17-19)

To show the contrast between these two ways of living, Paul lays out the difference between the ungodly and the godly. In the strongest language possible and with the authority of Christ, he gives us several reasons why we should not live like ungodly people.

They are hopelessly confused (4:17).

Those who live for themselves rather than Christ lose their godly perspective and start making poor decisions based on worldly thinking. Rather than drawing upon God's wisdom, they rely on human wisdom and rational thought. Nothing is wrong with thinking rationally, but when God is left out of the picture and the thinking is completely human-centered, it is futile. The ungodly may know about God, but they prefer to reinvent God into something that suits them (Romans 1:21). Even Christians can fall into the trap of worshiping the god they want rather than the God who is.

Their closed minds are full of darkness; they are far away from the life of God because they have shut their minds and hardened their hearts against him (4:18).

When confused thinking becomes the rule rather than the exception, ungodly people begin to shut their minds and harden their hearts to God. Literally, the ungodly live in a state of spiritual ignorance where "God has made them all look foolish and has shown their wisdom to be useless nonsense" (1 Corinthians 1:20). Be careful—this sad state of affairs can happen to Christians!

They don't care anymore about right and wrong, and they have given themselves over to immoral ways (4:19).

This is what happens when people drift away from God. They become desensitized to the things of God. Not all at once—this is a process that occurs over time. We heard about a young Christian man who became confused and subtly and secretly drifted away from God. Not even the guys in his accountability group knew what was going on. Then one day he announced that he was leaving his wife and kids. He didn't care anymore about doing the right thing, and his decisions had tremendous repercussions for the people around him.

Their lives are filled with all kinds of impurity and greed (4:19).

This is a pathetic way to live, but it's where the ungodly end up. They are on a slow progression down a reckless path. You might expect this of people who don't know God personally, but not of people who have been transformed by Jesus.

The Way the Godly Live (4:20-32)

Paul had heard that the Ephesian Christians were being lured by the culture. "But that isn't what you were taught when you learned about Christ," he writes. He then lays out several action steps for godly people who "have learned the truth that is in Jesus."

Throw off your old evil nature and your former way of life, which is rotten through and through, full of lust and deception (4:22).

This takes a deliberate choice—a daily one. Your "old evil nature" describes the person you were before you accepted Christ as your Lord and Savior. You don't just throw off the old nature once and expect it to leave you alone. That "old man" will come back to pester you and tempt you over and over again. Christ has given you a "new self." He crucified your "old self" on the cross (Romans 6:6). You need to live in the light of this reality.

Instead, there must be a spiritual renewal of your thoughts and attitudes (4:23).

The way to deal with your old sin nature is to cultivate a spiritual renewal of your thoughts and attitudes. Paul wrote to the Romans:

> *Don't copy the behavior and customs of this world, but let God transform you into a new person by changing the way you think. Then you will know what God wants you to do, and you will know how good and pleasing and perfect his will really is* (Romans 12:2).

God doesn't want you to live like an ungodly person. He wants to transform you by renewing your mind. That's why being engaged in systematic Bible study and being involved in regular fellowship with other maturing believers is so important for Christians at all levels of spiritual maturity. As you open your mind and your heart to the things of God, He will use the Holy Spirit to guide you (1 Corinthians 2:12).

You must display a new nature because you are a new person, created in God's likeness—righteous, holy, and true (4:24).

Think back to the shabby soldier in Alexander's army. When you display the old nature, you provide no evidence that you are a new person in Christ. And just how do you display your new nature? Not by being a spiritual phony. Your new nature flows from your right relationship with God, which will only come as you learn more and more about Him (Colossians 3:10).

So put away all falsehood and "tell your neighbor the truth" because we belong to each other (4:25).

Living in the body of Christ means we care about each other too much to lie to each other.

And "don't sin by letting anger gain control over you" (4:26).

You don't let anger gain control over you because you realize that Satan gets his claws most easily into angry people.

If you are a thief, stop stealing. Begin using your hands for honest work, and then give generously to others in need (4:28).

The godly person doesn't steal, but rather has a strong desire to engage in honest work. Furthermore, a godly person doesn't work just to get rich, but to give generously to others.

Don't use foul or abusive language. Let everything you say be good and helpful, so that your words will be an encouragement to those who hear them" (4:29).

You don't have to swear like a sailor to be guilty of using foul language. Someone who constantly criticizes others is also abusive. A godly person uses words that are good and helpful and encouraging to others.

Most of all, because you are letting the Holy Spirit have the run of your house, you do not "bring sorrow to God's Holy Spirit by the way you live" (4:30). You naturally want to "get rid of all bitterness, rage, anger, harsh words, and slander, as well as all types of malicious behavior" (4:31). Instead, you choose to "be kind to each other, tenderhearted, forgiving one another, just as God through Christ has forgiven you" (4:52).

Are you up for your mission to live like the godly person God wants you to be? Remember, this mission won't be accomplished in a short time, and you won't do it in your own strength. It's a lifelong mission that you can accomplish because you belong to Christ, because the Holy Spirit is your guarantee, and because you can share in God's power.

■ □ ■

Study the Word

1. Why do you think God designed the Christian life the way He did? Why do Christians still have to deal with the effects and the temptations of their old natures?

2. Have you ever been in a situation where your heart was hard to the things of God? How did you get into that place, and what did you do about it?

3. How does Ephesians 4:17-19 help you understand people who have not given their lives to Christ—why they think and act the way they do?

4. In Ephesians 4:20-32 Paul not only gives us a long list
    of attitudes and actions we are to get rid of but also
    gives us the attitudes and actions we are to incorpo-
    rate into our lives. In the space below, make a list of
    the ungodly characteristics we are to get rid of. Then,
    next to each one, list the godly qualities we are to
    incorporate.

    Get Rid Of...   **Incorporate...**

Which of these have you been challenged to deal
with recently? How is your progress coming along?

5. Read Ephesians 4:23 and Romans 12:2. List three things you can start doing today that will allow God to change the way you think.

6. Why is anger such a destructive force? Explain the difference between "righteous" or justifiable anger and anger that leads to sin.

7. Might someone be a thief without actually stealing physical property? How?

What does it mean to cheat God? (See Malachi 3:8-10.)

8. How is it possible to "bring sorrow to God's Holy Spirit by the way you live" (4:30)? (See 1 Thessalonians 5:19 and Titus 3:5.)

In what ways can you bring joy to the Holy Spirit?

Chapter 10

Open wide the windows of our spirits and
fill us full of light; open wide the door of our
hearts, that we may receive and entertain
Thee with all our powers of adoration.

—Christina Rosetti

You Have to *Choose*

In the final two chapters of Ephesians, Paul uses the technique of comparing opposites to illustrate the difference between godly and ungodly living. He compares light to darkness, wisdom to foolishness, and God's power to the power of darkness. In reality, there's no contest between these opposites. Light is always better than darkness, wisdom always beats foolishness, and God's power will always win over the powers of the enemy. But if you don't love the light, you won't know how bad the darkness is. If you don't seek wisdom, then foolishness will characterize your life. And if God's power doesn't fill you, the powers of evil will.

The Christian life isn't a zero sum game. You can't live your life between two opposites, hoping the two will balance each other out. You have to choose the way you want to live.

Loving the Light

Ephesians 5:1-20

*E*ach of us is the father of two children—a girl and a boy. They're all grown now and on their own, so we don't see them as much as we used to. But when we do get together with our respective families, we are often amazed at how much of ourselves we see in our kids. If you're a parent, you know what we're talking about. First, we see the physical resemblance between ourselves and our children (for some of our kids this is more of a curse than a blessing). But the similarities don't stop there.

When you observe your kids and realize that many of their personality traits and mannerisms are just like yours, you can be either amazed or unsettled (and sometimes both). The point is that we like to have our kids imitate our positive qualities.

Follow God's Example (5:1-2)

As chosen and adopted children of God, we need to view our relationship with our heavenly Father in the same way that we view our relationship with our earthly children. If you are pleased when your children imitate you, imagine how pleased God must be when we imitate Him. Because God is characterized by total goodness, amazing grace, and unconditional love, He is the best role model we can follow. God is the ultimate example.

Paul makes it clear that the best way to imitate God is to "live a life filled with love for others." God wants our lives to be characterized by love, and the best example we have is Jesus. When Jesus gave His life as a sacrifice to take away our sins, He pleased His Father. The love of Christ was like a "sweet perfume" to Him. In the same way, when we follow the example of Christ in love, we please God. "Our lives are a fragrance presented by Christ to God" (2 Corinthians 2:15).

Be Like Christ

Perhaps you saw the ad campaign telling you to "Be Like Mike." Well, we have a better idea: "Be Like Christ." When God sent Jesus to earth to die for us sinners, He showed us His ultimate love (Romans 5:8). But there was another reason Jesus came—so we could more easily imitate God. Jesus is God with skin on. He's "the visible image of the invisible God" (Colossians 1:15). Yes, Jesus died for you, but Jesus lived for you as well. He lived to show you how to live and how to love. If you want to follow God's example in all you do, study and imitate the life of Jesus. In other words, "Be Like Christ!"

After telling us to be like Christ, Paul lists some qualities that are the opposite of Christlikeness. These are the kinds of activities that people who live in darkness—people without Christ—routinely get involved with. Such sins should characterize neither the individual Christian nor the church. As individuals, we are God's new people (2 Corinthians 5:17). As members of the church, we are God's holy temple, joined together into one body (Ephesians 2:21). Anything we do to bring shame to ourselves and the body of Christ is unacceptable.

Stay Away from Sin (5:3-7)

Paul advises us to stay away from…

Sexual immorality, impurity, and greed (5:3)—These were tolerated in Roman society, as they are in our culture today. As Christians, we need to separate ourselves from such desires and activities.

Obscene stories, foolish talk, and coarse jokes (5:4)—Even if we don't engage in sexual immorality, we aren't off the hook. God doesn't even want us to talk about these things. Locker room humor, double entendres, bad language—"these are not for you." Too many Christians are too casual about their speech and joke-telling habits. We need to use our speech to thank God rather than demean people.

Can You Lose Your Salvation?

Paul comes down pretty hard on people who commit these sins and take them lightly. "You can be sure that no immoral, impure, or greedy person will inherit the Kingdom of Christ and of God," he says (5:5). Does this mean that people who do these things can't be saved or, if they are saved, they risk losing their salvation?

Obviously, sin is what separates us from God, and we can do nothing to earn our salvation. Only by God's special favor are we saved (2:8). On the other hand, once we are saved, nothing can separate us from the love of God (Romans 8:38).

What Paul is referring to here is a pattern of behavior that characterizes a life and continues without repentance. This could be true of an unbeliever, but a true Christian will repent and ask forgiveness if he or she is engaged in these kinds of sins. People who do not repent were probably not saved in the first place.

Love the Light (5:8-14)

Unrepentant people live in darkness. Even though we as Christians used to be in darkness, we are now "full of light from the Lord." Our behavior has to show it! Anytime we slip into an old sin habit, God's light in us is blocked out. For all practical purposes, we are in darkness, which is an awful place to be. The unbeliever can be quite comfortable in the darkness, but the Christian living there will be in pure misery.

You know what we're talking about. You've been there, and so have we. As children of light, we need to stay out of the darkness. And if we sin and stumble into the darkness, we can and should do only one thing :

This is the message he has given us to announce to you: God is light and there is no darkness in him at all. So we are lying if we say we have fellowship with God but go on living in spiritual darkness.... But if we confess our sins to him, he is faithful and just to forgive us and to cleanse us from every wrong (1 John 1:5-6,9).

$\mathcal{T}$he $\mathcal{L}$ight of the $\mathcal{L}$ord

One of the most consistent themes in the Bible is *light*. Notice how this image flows through Scripture:

- God's first command was, "Let there be light" (Genesis 1:3).

- The prophets predicted that a light would come to people in darkness (Isaiah 9:2).

- Jesus came to earth to be that light (John 1:9).

- Those who reject Jesus love darkness more than light (John 3:19).

- When Christ appears, His light will shine once again (2 Peter 1:19).

- In heaven there will be no sun, for the Son of God will be all the light we need (Revelation 21:23).

Live Wisely (5:15-20)

The Christian walk is characterized by wisdom, not foolishness. But wisdom doesn't come automatically. We need to ask God for wisdom (James 1:5), and we need to do wise things. Paul offers these suggestions:

Make the most of every opportunity (5:16).

You've heard the expression *Carpe diem!* It means "seize the day." That's what Paul is saying here. We need to seize each opportunity to serve Jesus and to please God, especially since we live in evil days. He's not encouraging us to be workaholics, but neither should we be lazy.

Try to understand what the Lord wants you to do (5:17).

Basically this means that we should try to understand the will of God. God's will is a mystery to many Christians, but it doesn't have to be. Most of what God wants us to do is found in His Word. As we study the Bible, God will reveal much of His will to us through the Holy Spirit. For those things not specifically found in Scripture, we need to pray diligently and associate with mature believers who can give us sound advice.

Let the Holy Spirit fill and control you (5:18).

Paul makes a contrast here between letting alcohol control you and letting the Holy Spirit control you. When a person gets drunk, we say he is "under the influence" of alcohol. Don't do this, Paul says. Instead, let the Holy Spirit influence you. Unlike the temporary high (and awful hangover) that alcohol produces, the Holy Spirit produces lasting joy. And just as a drunk is easy to spot, someone under the influence of the Holy Spirit will gain the attention of others:

- *A Spirit-filled person enjoys worshiping God (5:19).* When you are filled with the Spirit of God, you love to "sing psalms and hymns and spiritual songs."

- *A Spirit-filled person enjoys fellowship with other believers (5:19).* Praise and worship is more than a private activity. You regularly gather with other believers.

- *A Spirit-filled person is thankful (5:20).* The Bible commands us to "always be thankful" no matter what happens (1 Thessalonians 5:18). A thankful heart characterizes the life of a Spirit-filled Christian.

The Difference Between Baptizing and Filling

We got an e-mail from someone who wrote:

> The Bible says you have to be baptized by the Holy Spirit. Well, I haven't been, and I don't understand why. I study and read and go to church and talk to God, so why haven't I been baptized by the Holy Spirit yet?

This is a common misunderstanding many Christians have. They assume that being baptized by the Holy Spirit involves a special "laying on of hands" or "speaking in tongues." In fact, the Bible clearly teaches that when you accept God's gift of salvation through Jesus Christ, the Holy Spirit automatically baptizes you into the body of Christ (1 Corinthians 12:13). You don't have to do anything else. Being baptized by the Holy Spirit is part of the salvation benefits package, and it's a once-and-for-all event.

However, being *filled* by the Holy Spirit is not automatic. When Paul says that we should "let the Holy Spirit fill and control you," he's giving us a command. We have to give the Holy Spirit the run of our house and let Him control every part of our lives. If we have any unconfessed sin in our lives, the Holy Spirit can't fill us and He can't control us. When we confess our sins and ask forgiveness, we are cleaning our spiritual house, and the Holy Spirit can fill us completely.

■ ▢ ▢

Study the Word

1. You've heard the question, "What Would Jesus Do?"
   What does that mean in light of Ephesians 5:1-2 and
   1 John 2:6?

2. What does being a "sweet perfume" to God mean?
   We know that Jesus was a sweet perfume to God (5:2).
   How can we smell good to God as well? (See 2 Corin-
   thians 2:15.)

   How does this relate to Ephesians 5:2 and 5:10?

3. Read Ephesians 5:3-4. Are you being challenged in
   one of these areas?

   How seriously do most Christians take this warning?

What are the consequences of continuing to engage in this kind of spiritually risky behavior? (See Ephesians 5:6.)

4. The issue of eternal security—whether or not you can lose your salvation—is very troubling to many Christians. Do you agree or disagree with the conclusion in the box titled, "Can You Lose Your Salvation?" Why?

Can a person believe he or she is a Christian and in fact not be one?

5. Should the body of Christ judge or discipline a Christian who persists in living an unrepentant life? Use Scripture to support your answer.

6. Think back to when you lived in darkness. How long did you continue in this condition? How did you come out of the darkness and into the light?

7. Read Ephesians 5:15-18. How are you doing in each of the following areas?

   You are making the most of every opportunity.

   You are trying to understand what the Lord wants you to do.

   You are allowing the Holy Spirit to fill and control you.

8. Review the difference between being *baptized* by the Holy Spirit (1 Corinthians 12:13) and being *filled* with the Holy Spirit (Ephesians 5:18). List two benefits to each one.

Chapter 11

As believers, we are all called to servanthood
as an expression of our new life in Christ.

—*H. Norman Wright*

Respect Authority

Authority and submission are big issues in our culture today. Most people recognize that in any organization—whether it's a government, a company, or a family—someone needs to be in charge. But they don't always respect the authority that goes with the responsibility of leadership. So you have this constant tension between those who are called (or elected or appointed) to lead and those who are asked to follow.

Christians aren't immune to the temptation to rebel against authority. Rather than submitting to those who are over us, we are tempted to cling to what we think are our rights and demand equality. In this chapter we're going to deal with just one verse—Ephesians 5:21—and just one concept: submission. We want to put submission in its proper context before we talk about the various relationships where submission is required.

Loving Each Other
(Part 1)

Ephesians 5:21

---

*W*hat's *A*head

- ☐ The Biblical Context
- ☐ The Doctrinal Context
- ☐ The Relational Context
- ☐ The Cultural Context

*T*he section beginning with Ephesians 5:21 is one of the most controversial in all of Scripture, especially in our twenty-first-century world. From the seminary classroom to the church pew to the office watercooler, people are debating the meaning and application of these verses. What's all the fuss about? Mostly, it centers on the little word *submit,* particularly as it applies to wives and husbands. You want to start an argument? Quote this verse to a group of people and watch the fur fly:

> *You wives will submit to your husbands as you do to the Lord* (5:22).

For many people, this verse is bound in the ancient culture of the first-century Roman world. They think it doesn't apply to today's culture in which men and women are equal. Back in Paul's day, they reason, women were in a lower class than men, so they had to submit. This verse could not possibly be relevant to our liberated times, when everyone is equal.

Getting swept up in this kind of reasoning is easy, but the real answer is not that simple. Yes, considering the culture and historical context of any portion of Scripture is important (and we will do that a little later), but we can't simply interpret the Bible to fit our current social trends or political correctness. The meaning and application of God's Word is timeless. Whenever we come across a verse like Ephesians 5:22 or a passage like 5:21–6:9, we have to ask for wisdom as we diligently study its meaning and application to our lives. Most importantly, we need to discover the *context* in which the verse is written.

Context Rules

Whenever you read a book, a chapter, a verse, or even a word of Scripture, it must always be taken in *context,* which means "that which goes with the text." Context helps give meaning to the text you are studying. According to Kay Arthur, here's what you should ask yourself when you read the Bible: "Is my interpretation of a particular section of Scripture consistent with the theme, purpose, and structure of the book in which it is found?" That's context.

In addition, each book of the Bible has a different *historical* context, which has to do with the time and culture of the author and his readers. You have to ask *why* and *when* the book was written. Also, you should try to find out *what* was going on in the culture at the time, as well as *who* the major historical figures involved were. You can learn an amazing amount of information by studying the context of Scripture.

Let's look at how this passage of Scripture fits into the larger context. In this case, there are four different contexts:

The Biblical Context

Most Bible translations make a break after 5:21, which makes 5:22 the first verse you read in the next section. We think starting this section with 5:21 is important because it provides the context for everything that follows:

> *And further, you will submit to one another out of reverence for Christ* (5:21).

This is the overarching principle for the entire section that follows. Submission isn't a one-way street; it goes both ways. God is not asking one group of people to rule another. He is asking all of us to submit to one another. This is known as *mutual* submission, and it keeps these verses in the context of the entire book of Ephesians, which is all about God breaking down walls of hostility between people so we can live together as one body.

At the same time, the principle of submission is connected to the previous characteristics in 5:19-20, which in turn describe a person who is filled with the Holy Spirit (5:18). If you made a list of the qualities of a Spirit-filled person from this Bible passage, it would look like this:

- singing and making music to the Lord in your heart

- always giving thanks for everything to God

- submitting to one another out of reverence for Christ

The Doctrinal Context

The principle of submission has its roots in the heart of God. The reason we submit to each other is "out of reverence for Christ" (5:21). Jesus is our example in submission, and we are to follow Him. Christ's submissive attitude is eloquently expressed in Paul's letter to the Philippians:

> *Though he was God, he did not demand and cling to his rights as God. He made himself nothing; he took the humble position of a slave and appeared in human form* (Philippians 2:6-7).

Jesus gave up His rights. For our sake He took on the lowest possible position, that of a slave. His submission didn't make Jesus any less of a person. To the contrary, He was exalted because of it:

> *Because of this, God raised him up to the heights of heaven and gave him a name that is above every name* (Philippians 2:9).

Jesus Is God

This passage in Philippians is one of the clearest statements in Scripture supporting the doctrine that Jesus and God are one. When Paul wrote, "Though he was God," he was reinforcing this truth about Jesus: "For in Christ the fullness of God lives in a human body" (Colossians 2:9). If Jesus were not completely God, then His work on the cross would not have given us salvation. Paul states this fact about Jesus here in Ephesians as well. The phrase "out of reverence for Christ" is sometimes translated, "in the fear of Christ." Paul knew the Old Testament requirement to live "in the fear of God," so by saying "in the fear of Christ," Paul was affirming the deity of Jesus.

The doctrinal principle is that as Christians we need to follow the example of Christ and submit to one another instead of clinging to our rights.

The Relational Context

Paul follows his opening statement about mutual submission with three examples of human relationships: husbands and wives, parents and children, and masters and slaves. These basic relationships were found in the early church, and they exist today (except we have employers and employees rather than masters and slaves). "Moreover," writes Stott, "these three pairs of relationships are basic to all human existence."

Yes, Paul is calling for wives to submit to their husbands, for children to submit to their parents, and for slaves to submit to their masters. But in the biblical and doctrinal contexts, husbands, parents, and masters are not superior people. Wives, children, and slaves are not inferior, second-class citizens. We are all one in Christ. So, if that's the case, why does Paul ask one set of people to submit to another? The answer has to do with the way God designed us. Stott writes:

> The God of the Bible is a God of order, and in his ordering of human life (e.g., in the state and the family) he has established certain authority and leadership roles. And since such authority, though exercised by human beings, is delegated to them by God, others are required conscientiously to submit to it. Submission is a humble recognition of the divine ordering of society.

The Cultural Context

Okay, to this point you might still be a little uncomfortable with this whole submission business. Or you might be wondering, "What's the big deal?" Or you may think that everybody understands the concept of mutual submission. Not exactly. You see, in some homes and institutions in this country, people consider themselves better than others. In many countries on this planet, certain people with power rule over people who have no rights. Even in our "enlightened" twenty-first-century world, Paul's message that we should all submit to one another is progressive and beneficial.

But our culture is only part of the story. In the first-century Roman world, the message of mutual submission was so radical that the churches in Asia Minor probably couldn't believe what they were reading. Not only was the first-century world rigidly stratified, but women, children, and slaves were in the lowest class. *Women* were under the complete authority of men, especially in marriage. They were not equal to men, and they had few rights. Under Roman law, the father was supreme and *children* had no rights. Fathers could legally sell their children as slaves. And *slaves* were treated like things, not people. They were property to be bought and sold.

So when Paul called upon husbands to love their wives (5:25), fathers to treat their children fairly (6:4), and masters to treat their slaves well (6:9), this was truly revolutionary stuff. God has ordained that order and authority exist in society, but He also calls for love and respect for all people. *Authority* doesn't mean tyranny, and *submission* doesn't mean inferiority. The message of Ephesians and of the entire Bible is clear:

- All people have dignity before God because they have been created in His image (Genesis 1:27).

- All people are equal before God regardless of their race, class, and culture (Galatians 3:28).

- All Christians belong to one body as fellow members of God's family (Ephesians 4:4).

Jesus' Treatment of People

We've already seen that Jesus took on the role of a slave when He came to earth. Jesus also respected and honored women in a way that was unusual for His time. As for children, He said to His disciples, who wanted to send the children away, "Let the children come to me. Don't stop them! For the Kingdom of God belongs to such as these" (Luke 18:16). Jesus loved and liberated all people!

With these contexts in mind, let's take a look at the submission/authority dynamic in each of the three relationships. We'll do this in the next chapter.

■ ■ ■

*S*tudy the *W*ord

1. Why do you think the spiritual principle of submission has become such a hot and controversial topic in our culture?

2. How does the context of 5:21 change the way you view this verse and the passage that follows?

3. How does Christ's example of submission affect your willingness to submit to others?

4. Which translation affects you the most when it comes to your submission to others: "out of reverence for Christ" or "in the fear of Christ"? Why?

5. John Stott writes that "these three pairs of relationships"—husbands and wives, parents and children,
and masters and slaves—"are basic to all human existence." In the space below, make a list of your relationships next to each pair.

Husbands and wives

Parents and children

Masters and slaves

List one thing beside each relationship that you can do
to improve it.

6. What is your response to Stott's statement: "Submission is a humble recognition of the divine ordering of society"?

Is that statement hard for you to accept? Why or why not?

7. In what ways is submission expressed within the Trinity between the Father, the Son, and the Holy Spirit? Use Scripture to support your examples.

Do these acts of submission mean that any one of the Persons of the Godhead is not equal to the others?

Chapter 12

We have men who won't lead, women who won't follow, children who won't obey, and parents who won't nurture. It is every man for himself. The ship is going down, so every person is out to save his own neck.

—*Max Anders*

A Crisis of Authority

We have trouble submitting to the authority of others for many reasons: stubbornness, sin, and pride, just to name a few. None of these are valid excuses, but sometimes those in authority over us mistreat us and bring about feelings of rebellion and resentment. Husbands mistreat wives, parents abuse children, and employers cheat employees.

Some would say we have a crisis of authority in our culture, even to the highest echelons of leadership. Perhaps the abuse of power and the mistrust of leadership we are seeing on national and corporate levels have filtered down to the home and the family.

So what do you do? If you are in a place of authority, how are you supposed to lead? And if you are in a place where you need to submit, how do you do it without resentment? That's what we're going to talk about in this chapter.

Loving Each Other (Part 2)

Ephesians 5:21–6:9

*W*e can't emphasize enough how progressive and liberating Ephesians 5:21–6:9 is to every man, woman, and child living today, regardless of the culture. Unbelievers sometimes unfairly portray the Bible in particular and Christians in general as being provincial, out-of-date, and even tyrannical with regard to the basic human relationships described in this passage of Scripture. Some outspoken critics go so far as to say that the Bible demeans women and children and promotes slavery. Don't believe this errant thinking! Don't cave in to the culture. Know what the Bible really says about these issues. Know what you believe.

Authority and Submission

As we stated in the last chapter, nothing in this section of Ephesians—or the whole Bible, for that matter—promotes the demeaning, oppression, or mistreatment of one human being by another. Many people have unfortunately misinterpreted the Bible to promote their own misguided thinking. They prefer their own opinions to the truth of Scripture.

In fact, when you consider the life and actions of Jesus, who saw dignity in every person, regardless of sex, age, ethnicity, or social class, you can correctly conclude that the Bible and Christianity have set the standard of true liberation of the whole person—physically, mentally, and spiritually. John Stott writes:

> In the light of the teaching of Jesus and his apostles, we may confidently and repeatedly affirm at least three relevant truths: first, the *dignity* of womanhood, childhood, and servanthood; secondly, the *equality* before God of all human beings, irrespective of their race, rank, class, culture, sex, or age, because all are made in his Image; and the even deeper *unity* of all Christian believers as fellow-members of God's family and of Christ's body.

Because we can trust the teaching and example of Jesus regarding dignity, equality, and unity, we can also trust His teaching and example regarding authority and submission. As we consider the three sets of relationships in Ephesians 5:21–6:9, we will see that authority and submission are always in balance. Mutual submission looks like this:

- *Wives...submit to your husbands as you do to the Lord* (5:22).

- *And you husbands must love your wives with the same love Christ showed the church* (5:25).

- *Children obey your parents because you belong to the Lord, for this is the right thing to do* (6:1).

- *And now a word to you fathers. Don't make your children angry by the way you treat them* (6:4).

- *Slaves, obey your earthly masters, with deep respect and fear. Serve them sincerely as you would serve Christ* (6:5).

- *And in the same way, you masters must treat your slaves right...remember, you both have the same Master in heaven, and he has no favorites* (6:9).

Do you see the principle of mutual submission at work here? The principle of authority and submission must be in place in order for society and the family to function. But the principle won't work if it's one-sided. Let's take a look at how this principle works correctly in the three major relationships.

Wives and Husbands (5:22-33)

Wives are to submit to their husbands "as you do to the Lord." Paul isn't talking about rights here but about responsibilities. He uses the analogy of Christ and the church: Christ loves the church, and the church submits to Christ out of love. When a wife voluntarily submits to her husband, she is *not* subservient to him or less than he is. She is showing her submission to Christ.

A husband has an even greater responsibility before the Lord, and that's to love his wife. The word *love* here is *agape* love—it's a love that seeks out the highest good for the other person. This is "the same love Christ showed the church." Talk about a high standard! It's a sacrificial, caring, unbreakable love whereby the husband serves his wife. A wife can (and will even want to) submit to a husband who loves in this way because she's submitting to a lover, not a self-centered tyrant.

Children and Parents (6:1-4)

Open your local newspaper on any given day, and you're sure to find an article or two about child abuse. The way some parents treat their children is criminal. Yet here is a command in Scripture for children to obey their parents. Can parents abuse this command (as in "do as I say, not as I do")? Of course they can. This is not an absolute command. When a parent tells a child to do something illegal, unethical, or immoral, the child isn't obligated to obey. But in the proper context, obedience is necessary to keep order in the family and in society at large. In a very real sense, our social order and general safety depends on children's obedience to authority, beginning with their parents.

Just like wives and husbands, children and parents are to have a balanced relationship. Paul instructs fathers: "Don't make your children angry by the way you treat them" (6:4). No one said parenting was easy. It's the toughest job of all. What is easy is for a parent—especially a dad—to get frustrated and even angry at his kids. Being angry is okay, but sinning by letting anger gain control over you is never acceptable (4:26). Nothing discourages, angers, and builds resentment in children faster or more deeply than a father who disciplines in anger. On the positive side, fathers need to use godly discipline and instruction to raise emotionally healthy and spiritually maturing children.

Honor Your Father and Mother

Paul instructs children to not only obey their parents but to honor them as well. Obeying and honoring are two different things. In general children must obey their parents as long as they are living in their household. Honor goes beyond obedience, both in scope and in time. When you respect and love your parents no matter what, you are showing them honor, and this should never stop. God blesses those children who honor their parents throughout their lives.

Slaves and Masters (6:5-9)

Slaves have the same responsibility of submission to their masters as wives do to husbands and children do to parents. And the advice Paul gives to slaves applies to workers as well. So whether you feel like a slave in the company where you work, or you're trying to climb the ladder in a great corporation, Paul has some very practical advice.

Respect your employers and serve them as you would serve Christ. No matter where you are, live out your Christian life with love. Worry less about making yourself look good, and concentrate more on making your boss look good. Don't be a slacker. Work just as hard when the boss isn't looking as when he or she is because the Lord is always watching.

Masters have a responsibility before the Lord as well. If you're a boss of any kind—the shift manager at Taco Bell or the CEO of a Fortune 500 company—you need to respect your workers. Never threaten them, and always treat them the way Jesus treats you.

Slavery and the Bible

Why doesn't the Bible condemn slavery? The concept of one human being owning another like property is so disgusting that we can hardly imagine any circumstance in which it is an acceptable practice. Let's be clear about one thing. Although Paul doesn't condemn slavery, he doesn't condone it either. The reality is that in ancient times slavery was deeply instilled in the fabric of life. Barclay estimates that there were as many as 60 million slaves in the Roman Empire. Slaves were doctors, teachers, and administrators. In short, they did all of the work. That's one possible reason why Paul didn't call for an abolition of slavery. Stott gives two additional reasons. Slaves could win their freedom and become established in a trade or profession. That's why Paul wrote to the Corinthian church: "Are you a slave? Don't let that worry you—but if you get a chance to be free, take it" (1 Corinthians 7:21). Also, at the time Paul wrote his letters to the early churches, the laws regarding slavery were beginning to change. Reform was on the way. Nonetheless, Paul's words about a new relationship of mutual submission between slaves and masters made possible by Jesus Christ were revolutionary indeed.

What a beautiful picture of how human relationships should function when husbands and wives, parents and children, and masters and slaves relate in the way the Bible teaches. Order, harmony, and truth abound. And what a witness to the world! When you display this kind of biblical harmony and teamwork at home and at work, others will want to know the secret of your success. And you will be able to point to Christ, who showed us how to live.

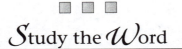

Study the Word

1. Is there a "crisis of authority" in any of your relationships? Explain.

2. Why might Ephesians 5:21–6:9 be subject to so much misinterpretation?

    Why is our culture today so unwilling to apply the truths in this passage as they relate to...

    husbands and wives

    parents and children

    masters and slaves

3. Give an example from Scripture where Jesus saw dignity in:

    women

    children

    slaves

4. How is the church's submission to Christ (5:23-24) a valuable example of a wife's submission to her husband?

    How is Christ's love for the church (5:25-27) a valuable example of a husband's love for his wife?

5. How can a child honor a parent who is abusive and unloving?

Does *honor* always mean *obey*? Why or why not?

6. The Greek word for *lovingly cares for* in 5:29 and the Greek word for *bring them up* in 6:4 are the same. What are the implications of this fact?

7. What is the practical application of this verse: "Work with enthusiasm, as though you were working for the Lord rather than for people" (6:7)?

On a scale of 1 to 10, how faithful have you been in your work habits and attitudes?

8. What does Paul mean in 6:9 when he says the Master in heaven "has no favorites"?

How might this change the way you live?

*C*hapter 13

Never lose sight of what God is doing through you, through the church. The world cannot see it, because the world is unaware of the heavenly realms. The world has no idea what is taking place through you and me, through the church. But you know what God is doing through you. His power surges through you. His love for the world flows out of you. His courage for the battle emboldens you. So do not lose heart. There's a war on—and you are on the winning side!

—*Ray Stedman*

Stand Firm

Paul closes his letter to the saints in Ephesus with a word of encouragement and a list of instructions for spiritual battle. The devil has all kinds of "strategies and tricks," which he doesn't hesitate to use. We must never forget that Satan is very real, and he doesn't play fair as he tries to destroy unbelievers and immobilize believers.

The good news in all of this is that Satan's power is limited but God's power is limitless.

> *But you belong to God, my dear children. You have already won your fight with these false prophets, because the Spirit who lives in you is greater than the spirit who lives in the world* (1 John 4:4).

So read on and learn how to stand firm against the dark forces of the unseen world.

Using the Armor of God

Ephesians 6:10-24

*P*eople didn't use to think about the devil much, and if they did, their mental images were comical. The cartoon version of Satan included a red suit, horns, and a pointy tail (oh, and let's not forget the trident). Or you had the Flip Wilson version of Satan. Anytime you made a mistake you could say, "The devil made me do it!"

Unbelievers still don't give Satan much thought (unless they are interested in the occult), but Christians these days tend to take the Prince of Darkness more seriously. One reason for this recent awareness is a novel called *This Present Darkness*, written by Frank Peretti in 1986. In graphic detail Peretti painted an unseen yet very real world inhabited by demons and angels who battle for the hearts and minds of mortals. Even Christians are not beyond the demonic influences of Satan and his hoards. (Another great book that will give you some useful insights into the ways of Satan and his demons is *The Screwtape Letters* by C.S. Lewis.)

We think *This Present Darkness* is an inspired piece of work. However, we should not have needed a novel to tell us the truth about the "evil rulers and authorities" and the "mighty powers of darkness" from the unseen world "who rule this world." They are mentioned right here in Ephesians 6:10-20.

Be Strong with God's Power (6:10-12)

This passage on "this present darkness" may seem a bit out of place in Ephesians, especially after Paul's instructions regarding mutual submission. But taken in the context of the entire letter, it is completely in line with the third major theme of Ephesians: We can share in God's power.

Whether we are striving against sin, struggling to submit to one another, or standing firm against the strategies and tricks of the devil, we need God's power. And He gladly gives it to us. This isn't a Harry Potter "wave your wand and make fire" kind of make-believe power. God's supernatural power is more like spiritual body armor, and it's very real.

The reality is that we face a spiritual enemy. We may think that certain people are against us, but people are hardly a threat compared to the real enemy. Our battle is against "wicked spirits in the heavenly realms." There are demons who tempt us to sin and cosmic powers that try to control the world. This formidable army of darkness is desperate to thwart God's plan of redemption through Jesus Christ and the church.

We shouldn't panic in the face of this opposition because we know how the last chapter ends. We are assured of victory through Jesus Christ our Lord. But we need to take our enemy seriously. Satan and his evil followers have kidnapped this planet, and until Christ returns to take charge once again, we must resist the devil with God's mighty power.

Satan Is Everywhere

Satan is not omnipresent—that is, he is not everywhere at once as God is—but he gets around quite effectively. When Paul warns us about "the evil rulers and authorities of the unseen world" who "rule this world" and who exist "in the heavenly realms" (6:12), he is showing us the full reach of Satan's presence and the full extent of his warfare.

Use Every Piece of God's Armor (6:13-17)

We are in a spiritual battle, so we have to use spiritual weapons. We can thank God that He has already prepared an incredible suit of spiritual armor for us to use. All we have to do is put it on and use every piece. Paul describes God's armor in detail:

The belt of truth (6:14)—For the Roman soldier, the leather belt was the foundation for the rest of the armor. It held other weapons and kept everything in place. For the Christian, the belt of truth is the truth of Scripture. We must know the Word of God and stand on its truths if we are to resist the devil. Even Jesus needed the Word of God to resist Satan's temptations.

The body armor of God's righteousness (6:14)—Body armor consisted of a large leather or bronze breastplate that protected the vital organs from attack. It was a defensive piece of equipment. God's righteousness is our defense against Satan's accusations. Because of what Christ did for us on the cross, we are righteous before God. Living every day as righteous people, pleasing God in all we do, is an effective defense in our spiritual battle.

The shoes of peace (6:15)—Shoes are incredibly important to a soldier. Unless his feet are protected, he can't walk. Unless he is surefooted, he will stumble. Paul uses this imagery to show us that peace comes from the Good News. We need to understand what we believe in order to be ready in all situations.

The shield of faith (6:16)—Roman soldiers used their shield to deflect arrows and other offensive weapons. The powers of darkness are constantly sending arrows of temptation and doubt our way to get our attention away from Christ. We need to take up the shield of faith in order to resist. We need to trust God completely in all situations.

The helmet of salvation (6:17)—Paul instructs us to "put on" the helmet of salvation that God has given us by His grace. A helmet protects the head, so you could say that God's salvation protects our minds. Salvation isn't just something that happens to us. It is the transformational power of God, and we need to take hold of it with our minds as well as our hearts. When we know for sure that we are saved, we can stand against Satan's blows to our head, which come in the form of twisted ideas and doubts.

The sword of the Spirit (6:17)—This is the only offensive weapon Paul mentions, and it's a powerful one. The sword of the Spirit is the Word of God, described in

Hebrews as "full of living power" and "sharper than the sharpest knife" (Hebrews 4:12). We need the Holy Spirit to help us use the Word of God for all it's worth, but first we must know it. Your Bible won't do you much good if it's sitting on the shelf collecting dust. The most effective way to resist temptation and the tricks of Satan is to know the Word of God.

A Soldier in *T*raining

All God's spiritual armor and weaponry won't do you much good if you don't know how to use it, and the only way you will know how to use God's armor is to put yourself in a spiritual training program. You need to study your Bible systematically, pray daily, attend a Bible-teaching church regularly, and serve others continuously. As Paul advised Timothy, "Work hard so God can approve you" (2 Timothy 2:15).

Pray at All Times (6:18-20)

Paul closes this section with a plea for the Christians in Ephesus and beyond to pray. Although prayer is not mentioned as one of the pieces of God's armor, it definitely belongs in the spiritual arsenal. Prayer is not a weapon but rather a way to invoke the power of God for ourselves and others. We need to pray for Christians everywhere, and we need to pray especially for those who are actively taking the Good News into the world. Specifically, we need to...

- *Pray at all times and on every occasion.* This doesn't mean that all you do is pray. But you need to have an attitude of prayer at all times.

- ***Pray in the power of the Holy Spirit.*** Our "unceasing" prayers must be empowered by the Spirit of God.

- ***Pray persistently.*** Don't get weary in your praying. Keep at it.

Epilogue (6:21-24)

Paul closes this wonderful letter with a word of encouragement. His messenger, Tychicus, will encourage the believers by telling them that Paul is doing well despite his circumstances. Paul then gives his readers a blessing of peace, love, and grace from God the Father and the Lord Jesus Christ.

We hope you have been encouraged as you have studied the book of Ephesians. Our prayer for you is that you would know that you belong to Christ, that the Holy Spirit is your guarantee, and that you can share in God's mighty power.

■ ▦ ▣

Study the Word

1. Can Christians think too little of Satan? Can they think too much? What are the disadvantages of each way of thinking?

2. Why do you think God continues to let Satan rule this world? Why doesn't God just put an end to Satan and evil right now?

3. Far fewer people believe in the existence of Satan and hell than in the existence of God and heaven. Why do you think this is?

4. Paul is no advocate of passive Christianity. In Ephesians 6:11-14 he tells us to...

- be strong (6:10)

- stand firm (6:11)

- resist the enemy (6:13)

- stand firm (6:13)

- stand your ground (6:14)

List some practical ways you can be a proactive Christian by heeding Paul's advice.

5. Why do you think Paul used the analogy of a suit of armor to describe the way we need to stand firm against Satan and his demons?

6. Review the six pieces of armor. Do you have any "chinks" in your armor? Where are you vulnerable?

7. Okay, you're all suited up with God's armor. How do you actually fight your spiritual battles?

Dig Deeper

*W*henever we write a book about God and His
Word, we do a lot of research and reading. Here
are the main books we used to write this study on Ephesians. If you want to dig deeper into Ephesians and the
Bible, here's a great place to start.

Commentaries

Max Anders is the editor of an excellent series called the
Holman New Testament Commentary. He wrote the commentary called *Galatians, Ephesians, Philippians & Colossians*.

One of our favorite New Testament Bible scholars is
William Barclay. He's down-to-earth yet deep (a rare com-
bination). We used his book, *The Letters to the Galatians and
Ephesians* from The Daily Study Bible Series.

J. Vernon McGee is another great Bible teacher. We
relied on *Ephesians* from his Thru-the-Bible Commentary
Series.

The Life Application Bible Commentary series is out-
standing, and *Ephesians* was a big help.

The Message of Ephesians by John R.W. Stott is from the commentary series called The Bible Speaks Today. This one is a little deeper than the others, but still understandable.

The New Testament volume of *The Bible Knowledge Commentary,* edited by John Walvoord and Roy Zuck, provides valuable background and historical information.

Likewise, the New Testament volume of *The Bible Background Commentary* by Lawrence Richards is a great Bible study tool.

Two other single volume commentaries we routinely use are the *Matthew Henry Commentary* and *The Wycliffe Bible Commentary.*

General Bible Study Helps

Now don't laugh, but two books on the Bible we found helpful in writing the study of Ephesians are by…well, *us!* Check out *Bruce & Stan's Guide to the Bible* and *Bruce & Stan's Pocket Guide to Studying Your Bible.* They are written in the same "user-friendly" style as this book.

Three books gave us very useful historical and personal information on the apostle Paul: *Life and Letters of Paul* by Dana Gould, *Desire of the Everlasting Hills* by Thomas Cahill, and *Who's Who in Christian History* by J.D. Douglas.

Bible Translations

Obviously you can't study Ephesians or the Bible without the primary source—the Bible! People often ask us, "Which Bible translation should I use?" We recommend that your primary study Bible be a *literal* translation (as opposed to a paraphrase), such as the *New International Version* (NIV) of the Bible or the *New American Standard Bible* (NASB). However, it's perfectly acceptable to use a Bible paraphrase, such as *The Living Bible* or *The Message* in your devotional reading.

Our personal choice for Bible study is the *New Living Translation* (NLT), a Bible translation that uses a method called "dynamic equivalence." This means that the scholars who translated the Bible from the original languages (Hebrew and Greek) used a "thought for thought" translation philosophy rather than a "word for word" approach. It's just as accurate but easier to read. In the final analysis, the Bible that's best for you is the Bible you enjoy reading because you can understand it.

A Word About Personal Pronouns

When we write about God, we prefer to capitalize all personal pronouns that refer to God, Jesus, and the Holy Spirit. These would include *He, Him, His,* and *Himself.* However, not all writers follow this practice, and there's nothing wrong with that. In fact, personal pronouns for God were not capitalized in the original languages, which is why you'll find that the Bible uses *he, him, his,* and *himself.*

Bruce and Stan would enjoy hearing from you. The best ways to contact them are...

Snail mail: Twelve Two Media,
PO Box 25997
Fresno, CA 93729-5997

E-mail: info@christianity101online.com

Web site: www.brucebickel.com

Christianity 101® Series

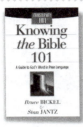

Knowing the Bible 101
Enrich your interaction with Scripture with this user-friendly guide, which shows you the Bible's story line and how each book fits into the whole. Learn about the Bible's themes, terms, and culture, and find out how you can apply the truths of every book of the Bible to your own life.

Creation & Evolution 101
With their distinctively winsome style, Bruce Bickel and Stan Jantz explore the essentials of creation and evolution and offer fascinating evidence of God's hand at work. Perfect for individual or group use.

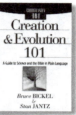

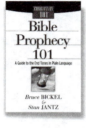

Bible Prophecy 101
In their contemporary, down-to-earth way, Bruce and Stan present the Bible's answers to your end-times questions. You will appreciate their helpful explanations of the rapture, the tribulation, the millennium, Christ's second coming, and other important topics.

Knowing God 101
This book is brimming with joy! Whatever your background, you will love the inspiring descriptions of God's nature, personality, and activities. You will also find straightforward responses to the essential questions about God.

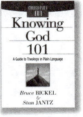

Growing as a Christian 101
In this fresh new look at the essentials of the Christian walk, Bruce Bickel and Stan Jantz offer readers the encouragement they need to continue making steady progress in their spiritual lives.

Word Religions and Cults 101
This study features key teachings of each religion, quick-glance belief charts, biographies of leaders, and study questions. You will discover the characteristics of cults and how each religion compares to Christianity.

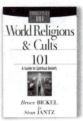

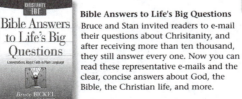

Bible Answers to Life's Big Questions
Bruce and Stan invited readers to e-mail their questions about Chrisitanity, and after receiving more than ten thousand, they still answer every one. Now you can read these representative e-mails and the clear, concise answers about God, the Bible, the Christian life, and more.

Christianity 101® Bible Studies

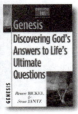

Genesis: Discovering God's Answers to Life's Ultimate Questions

"In the beginning" says it all. Genesis sets the stage for the drama of human history. This guide gives you a good start and makes sure you don't get lost along the way.

1 & 2 Corinthians: Finding Your Unique Place in God's Plan

This enlightening study explores the apostle Paul's helpful responses to issues that churches continue to face today: maintaining unity in the church, exercising spiritual gifts, and identifying authentic Christian ministry.

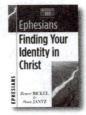

John: Encountering Christ in a Life-Changing Way

This study reveals who Jesus is by demonstrating the dramatic changes He made in the lives of the people He met, including Nicodemus, the woman at the well, Lazarus, and John, "the disciple whom Jesus loved."

Ephesians: Finding Your Identity in Christ

Verse for verse, the book of Ephesians is one of the most profound, powerful, and practical books in the Bible. This guide reveals the heart of Paul's teaching on the believer's identity in Christ.

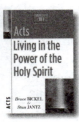

Acts: Living in the Power of the Holy Spirit

Bruce and Stan offer a fresh look at the ongoing ministry of Jesus through the church. They highlight the drama of the early Christians' triumph over darkness and their explosive growth from a band of 120 fearful followers to a thriving, worldwide church.

Philippians/Colossians: Experiencing the Joy of Knowing Christ

This new 13-week study of two of Paul's most intimate letters will inspire you to know Christ more intimately and maintain your passion and vision. Filled with helpful background information, up-to-date applications, and penetrating, open-ended questions.

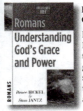

Romans: Understanding God's Grace and Power

Paul's letter to the church in Rome is his clearest explanation and application of the good news. This fresh new study of Romans assures you that the Gospel is God's answer to every human need.

Revelation: Unlocking the Mysteries of the End Times

Have you ever read the final chapters of the Scriptures, only to finish with more questions than answers? Bruce and Stan help you understand Revelation's encouraging message and apply it to your life today.

Exclusive Online Feature

Here's a Bible study feature you're really going to like!
Simply go online at:

www.christianity101online.com

There you'll find a Web site designed exclusively for users of the Christianity 101 Bible Studies series. Just click on the book you are studying, and you will discover additional information, resources, and helps, including...

- *Background Material*—We can't put everything in this Bible study, so this online section includes more material, such as historical, geographical, theological, and biographical information.

- *More Questions*—Do you need more questions for your Bible study? Here are additional questions for each chapter. Bible study leaders will find this especially helpful.

- *Answers to Your Questions*—Do you have a question about something in your Bible study? Post your question and an "online scholar" will respond.

- *FAQ's*—In this section are answers to some of the more frequently asked questions about the book you are studying.

What are you waiting for? Go online and become a part of the Christianity 101 community!